CW00881339

# THE *Rose* OF
# HARLEM

*21 short stories
about New Yorkers*

PERE ORTÍS

ARCHWAY
PUBLISHING

Archway Publishing books may be ordered through booksellers or by contacting:

Archway Publishing
1663 Liberty Drive
Bloomington, IN 47403
www.archwaypublishing.com
1 (888) 242-5904

ISBN: 978-1-4808-9329-0 (sc)
ISBN: 978-1-4808-9327-6 (hc)
ISBN: 978-1-4808-9328-3 (e)

Library of Congress Control Number: 2020913402

Print information available on the last page.

Archway Publishing rev. date: 07/30/2020

The citizen of the Great Apple is presented, through the twenty-two New York short stories included in this book, confronted to the different situations and eventualities of the urban life as a diluted protagonist in the *tremens melting pot,* selected at random in all the metropolitan ambient, upon the massive and depersonalizing magma. The personages become varied models which reflect the unclassifiable psychology of the New Yorker. With a clear and meaningful language the author questions himself what else could do, in the aggressive context if they are human beings... It would be different if they wore dresses of the gods! The lector will find in these stories amenity, surprise and unexpected horizons.

(Beside the photo:) Pere Ortís was born in Catalonia in 1930. He studied there his bachelor career and completed his studies in NYU. He has lived for thirty years in the area of New York City and resided, before, twelve years in Honduras, C.A. Both places have been a great inspiration for him. Ortís is the author of nineteen novels, in Catalan, plus three books of short stories, this one about New York, another about Honduras and the third about Urgell, his County in Catalonia, five books of essays, specially about Catalan nationalist subjects, three travel books, four books about the Catalan language, and several translations from English into Catalan, and from Catalan into English. He publishes essays in a couple of local magazines

Translated from Catalan into English by the author himself.

(Motto:) *Yes, if you were gods, you could be ashamed of your dresses.*

*In this way Zarathrusta spocke.* Friedich Wilhem Nietzsche.

Dedicated to all those who helped me to learn the English language, when I came to New York City.

# Contents

# The man who believed he was Dos Passos

*A* flagrant case of double personality, but may be merely ghostly and of pure mental inanity. Anyway, the interested one needed to prove it. He was sure he had a bunch of reasons in his hand to prove it.

The subject –it was necessary to distinguish him with names of an abstraction, as *the man, the one, the individual, the subject,* because such names referred more strongly to his uncertain condition– since he ignored what his name was and, departing from the patronymic gap he jumped to the conclusion that he at least was a reincarnation of the eminent writer, or maybe he was a clone of his, maybe he was the invention of some scientist who was making scientific experiments at random, and at last he got it in his person. "Because", he used to argue, "all his life as an infant and an adolescent was sunk in the darkness of a total amnesia and just kept conscience of himself since his life of an adult, being this generated by a monothematic identification

1

with the endeavor, the mind, the work and sickliness, both physic and moral, of the great novelist". And he added: "Always I talk to the scientists and to the doctors about the obviousness of this condition of my person, they do not take it seriously and scape from my confidence, ashamed because my case goes beyond all their previsions and their theories, being they as much scientific as they want to be, yet being unable to grasp my reality", the subject affirmed with great conviction.

"You fixed this nonsense to your brains after the indigestions produced to you by the excessive readings of Dos Passos", a distinguished doctor of the team of Mount Sinai Hospital smashed to his face, by the way a specialist in the more acute cases of a double personality.

"I never read but a single book of Dos Passos!" the man refused to admit his opinion, with an objectivity that nobody could refuse. "I don't know any title from him. Nevertheless, I guaranty I can recite full paragraphs of any of his writings, right away the one you point me out", the man proposed to him.

The specialist of Mount Sinai made a grimace of skepticism in front of that declaration, since it seemed so ridiculous to him

"Come on, these are pure fantasies of yours, don't come to me with these nonsenses!" he answered back to him, willing to finish with the question, the so frequent resource of vilifying the opinion of the others. "Feed yourself sanely with other varied readings and you'll see how these so absurd ideas fade out from your mind!"

"Because what I say does not fit your material interests and your ridiculous mentality, did not pay attention to what I said: I never read a single book of his!" the subject replied very angry. "How do you intent to judge in the case, if you despise this so elementary circumstance?"

The specialist took this refusal with the same passive routine he took the botches of the inmates which not rarely his patients flocked him in the section of psychiatry of the hospital. He shrugged his shoulders and let the man alone because, in the long run, he was not any danger to the public health.

But he later on gave another thought to it. He was having lunch with his wife and the look given to him, from the television screen, by a sheep cloned by some British scientists remembered him the talk he held in the morning with the maniac subject. That vague look, steamed up with a dim origin, but out of question addressed precisely to his person, worried him with the idea of the genetic mystery hidden in that *man* and at least made him understand a bit of his own struggle in the research of his personal identity.

"The struggle to find your own identity is the most painful and insomniac thorn that a human being can have pricked in his soul in this uncertain life", he was saying at table ruminating in a loud voice, not caring about his wife, whom he considered not able to reach the highness of his psychiatrists lucubrations. (((if not lucubrations: fantasies)))

"I believe it", she agreed any way, soaking the mare of a turkey bone, like she was trying to get the psychiatry of the species. "For this reason, my dear, it is very convenient you apply your best efforts to elucidate this case. It is so important that you can play the high scientific clarinet at the end of the millennium; you may become famous. To be distinguished with the Nobel Prize of the best scientist in the world, imagine!

"The issue of your identity is unique in importance! Here is the ideal of all the religions, of all the philosophies, of all the hidden sciences, this question of where you come from, who are you, what are you doing in this world, where are you going…", he continued divagating, placing the words of his wife in the shadow, as a simple background music, in spite that they always had more practical sense than his own words. (His wife was faithful in love to him, to the extent of getting to a level of a kind of ideological masochism toward the husband's opinions adverse to the more logical and vital feminism).

"And don't save the means working for it! Neither save the persons, get advantage of your position and of your connections"she was encouraging him being an expert in that conjugal Machiavellism which conducted him wherever she wanted.

Since this introverted dialogue, the doctor had no rest thinking about how he could find the explanation of the hidden motive which that guy was keeping in his brains, for the good of him and of himself, since the theme was keeping him disquiet and was secreting such an unrest equal to his professional fiasco, it's to say, like a pragmatic inanity as a psychiatric, afraid that it could be noticed by his wife, which could vex him as much as a sexual impotence. The matter was pressing him in a dirty, abusive way.

Prone to spent his nights in blank, shaken by the abstruse of a really crazy patient, at dawn he had taken a very definite resolution: he would go to ask the help of a confident in his skepticism which both were keeping in reference to many historical figures that caused more impact about the inscrutable human impressionability. They say that Saint George is a product of a popular twaddle. Who guarantees us that Joan of Arc is a real fairy out of the imagination of the French, reckless by a war they were losing?

"I got the case of a psychic sub product tormented because he believes he is a clone of Dos Passos", he said to the friend, after the uncomfortable night thinking about it.

His friend listened to it with his open eyes. He was Mr. George Fromm, a former director of a famous university, a hypochondriac type and, in several cases, he showed an aggressive rudeness.

"Very interesting!" he muttered, according to his way of getting into intricate considerations of an obscure fever. "This is an excellent field to submerge yourself in waves of doubts which take away from you the sensation of the passing by time".

He was the most outstanding in the themes of Dos Passos,

beyond being a personal acquaintance of the great writer and having had literary contacts with him. He wrote his doctoral thesis about the famous Americanized Lusitanian: *Tics of atavism in the anthropologic visions of "Manhattan Transfer", deriving from the Lusitanian fauna.* The one of Mount Sinai hatred to death his hypochondriac temperament, but in spite of it he had no choice but asking his help. They were sincere enemies, to say it exactly as it was, but they could not do one without the other.

"Please, you just localize him for me and I'll take care of the rest", he proposed to the one from Mount Sinai. "I'll be alone with him and, with much subtlety, I'll mention him *Three Soldiers* or *Manhattan Transfer,* and see what kind of a reaction he makes to it".

And this proposition did not please the other one. Suddenly this one considered himself running the risk of losing the privilege that could become a hen of the golden eggs in his favor... And he got ready to watch it. He forgot about the hypochondriac teacher, and would be very careful not to let the rain of the case get away from his hand.

At the time to localize the subject in the infinite ambient of the city, he went straight to meet him seated in one of the benches of Rockefeller Center, where Dos Passos seated many times to fish "physiognomies" for his *Manhattan Transfer.*

Nevertheless, he did not approach him at once, while the subject was looking at the different and numerous faces, as Dos Passos did, by the way the subject doing it with little precaution with the young girls, and the prettiest ones, who frequently felt in their skins the dart of those eyes and dedicated him a grunt of satisfaction.

The one from Mount Sinai rushed to meet the one from that university and they both approached with much precaution to that bench. To their luck the subject was still seated in the same bench, in Rockefeller Center, and was busy in the task of looking at the different faces, mainly of young women. Surely both scrutinized him with some fever.

"Hum...!" the one from the university mumbled in front of that subject.

And the one from Mount Sinai experienced a cold surprise because that "Hum...!" left him totally in blank.

"You wait in this place and I will approach him in order to catch him by surprise", the one from the university imposed on the other. I will use my best psychological abilities and suddenly I'll pour into him *The Three Soldiers...* It has to be something very subtle and verified by just one mind, do you understand?

The nameless, as he had gotten the psychological scent of that "Hum...!" got up from the seat and entered a cafeteria. Not being aware of their presence, of course. He took some food from the bar and sat at a table, ready to appease his hunger.

When he saw the strange coming toward himself, he did not move or shake at all, yet kept chewing normally. The other bent his head to him and excused himself to seat next to him in the same table, since the others seemed to be all taken. And the new comer started talking to him, in an innocent attitude.

The one from Mount Sinai was watching what was going on in that table from some distance, behind a glass door, and he was not missing any small detail, since his life depended on the developments over there. He was upset because he could not grasp any word of what was spoken in that table. What he said before "I'll use my best psychological abilities" was keeping him in a bothersome alert and he was imagining that it was an unforgivable usurpation of his best professional attributions.

Notwithstanding, the interview of the one from Columbia did not last that long. He shook hands with the nameless and came back to the rear of the glass door with an expression in his face which caused a severe impression in the other.

"This guy has surely fooled you!" he smashed to his face,

unpleasant and acid, as the one who sees his peace in the retirement is taken by trifles that are not wordy of any consideration. "This poor element could never be Dos Passos, don't make confusions! Because Dos Passos hated the hamburger with *ricolla* cheese and always refused the pumping pie, as a desert. Besides, he wore precious glasses of tortoiseshell and this miserable beggar does not go beyond using a simple *Truman*.

This report crushed the one from Mount Sinai. The triumph of his friend upon the most refined aspect of his business, altered him a lot. He underwent a short psychological flash that made available for him the solution of committing suicide.

Since those facts, a biological emptiness was established as far as the *nameless* was concerned. The guy who had awaked the greatest attention in the prestigious institutions of Mount Sinai and the university, and licked up the glory of an interesting discovery in his person, fell into the abyss of indifference and of intentional oblivion, as it is done with an obstacle or with an old useless piece of furniture which may bring you to the public ridiculousness. This fact could not be missed by the guy without name, since it was the equivalent to the official negation of his eminent identity. He guest all of it with a brightness that hurt him.

Though he –*the man, the subject, the nameless*– found the impulse to get up again in his fall. Surely he would impose his truth to all those so learned and wise who were denying his great identity with the famous novelist and were pitying him as a dreamer and easily deceived as a retarded one. He never met physically Dos Passos and only had an idea of how he was by a photo in the British Encyclopedia. So he possessed a diaphanous vision of his physiognomy, of his facial traits, of his illustrious boldness, of his expressions of deputy in the Parliament expressed by the rare combination of the tortoiseshell glasses and hairy eyebrows. He would do away with the proud erudite who were dealing with his privilege in such a lecherous manner.

A few days after what had happened in the restaurant of Rockefeller Center, he visited the Wax Museum of the City and after a short strategic period observing Abraham Lincoln and Marilyn Monroe, and verifying that the visitors were not paying any attention to him as something extraordinary, he stepped in an empty stool between the figures of William Faulkner and Edgar Allan Poe, which stool surely belonged to Al Capone, who possibly had been removed from there in order to repair his face of a bully after some facial scratch produced by some nail adverse to mafia. The nameless was wearing gray trousers and a gray jacket which had many white dots, a tie of a neutral color too worn and a shirt with a tore down collar, with no elegance at all; he placed an artificial baldness upon his abundant hair, put some amount of liquid wax in all his body, and wore the tortoise shell glasses, to end up by presenting a face of a dead person, yet alive by that smile of a diplomatic of a *Banana Republic* which was characteristic in the face of Dos Passos –what means that he came to the museum with the idea of doing it. Besides he heard those two guys commenting that they were coming the following morning to the Wax Museum to check the statue of Dos Passos. He wrote this name in a small piece of cardboard and put it into his pocket, until tomorrow, he fixed it in his chest, inserted in a bottom of the jacket. The visitors of the museum were moving beneath him as he was there long time ago or maybe looking at him in a routine glance, the majority ignoring the existence or the name of the famous writer.

And this was happening until the nameless could enjoy a recondite *vendetta*. The gods were benign to him! He discovered, among the tourists, the former director of the university, Mr. George Fromm, and the one from Mount Sinai, with the evident intention of scrutinizing him at a short distance. They were coming to take a "clinic" glance from him in the Wax Museum, shortly after the official restoration of the statue of Dos Passos.

They approached him and they both looked at him with a great interest. The former director of the university opened his mouth after a while:

"That poor beggar just confused me, surely. You have here the perfect image of the novelist Dos Passos, don't make any confusion about it! There is not some dreamer who could falsify it, no way! My Country persuades me of his degree of civilization by its fidelity to remember and to value the geniuses who made it great".

And at this point, the one from Mount Sinai, while scrutinizing the wax statue, stepped back, pushed by a dreadful shock, and started perspiring coldly. To fix his tormented eyes in the eyes of the one from the university, who was still scrutinizing the profile of the statue. The glance of the one from Mount Sinai was the announcement of a temperamental outburst…

# Blood on the asphalt

The hardened drunkards gather in the side of the sun of the Bowery, on the winter season, and in its shadow, during summer, from immemorial times. They make the zone typical with their *Pierrot* noses, by their brambled beards, by their scalding eyes and their beatific faces. Upon the side walk they profess the religion of helping the brother with some coin, when he has none to favor his anxiety for another drink, as an example of brotherhood and of good will toward your equal. They support each other, they fight, they argue without any theme, they fight for the sib of scotch and share it in the middle of dreadful looks and mellifluous glances. Some of them reach the mystic of this religion lying in their backs in the sidewalk upon the violent pool of a delirium tremens. At this moment one can see the flashes of the cameras of the tourists and of spirited drivers who pass by speeding in an auto mobile, surely aggressive toward the indifferent and restful citizen.

This section of the Bowery is a land mark of those who want to explore, under a personal initiative, the promised land of those to whom the drinking habit has isolated from their relatives and from their neighbors, a land that flows honey and milk of the organic juices upon the pavement of the street and the sidewalk, where old, dry, solid animal odors have been stacked. The more constructive ones come here to find Dickens' faces, for their psychological analysis, to increase their collection of horrible looks and to get physiognomies for magazine and novels of the black gender, magazines of the heart and of other colors.

Audrey Palmer acts as a leader and despot upon the group living in the city open, as to say the group living in the urban countryside. He is a learned guy, expert and talented to the extent of selecting the kind of alienation he was adopting to do away with the specter of the financial fiascos which lately have crushed him. Consequently, he promotes the excess of spirits in the ambient of his brains, in spite of having been a former progressive politician and more clever than the rest, advanced to his time. He had been condemned by the experts in the state corruption which, by the way he planned to combat by the hunger clamor of the poor. He was minister of economy in his Latin Country –or maybe in his Scandinavian Country, because his actual name is a pseudonym in substitution of the genuine one for state reasons–, and as soon as they saw him fallen into the pit of drunkenness and despised by the well-to-do people, even his wife betrayed him with a minister who was flattering the powerful and was taking her to the reunions of a diplomatic character.

The man celebrated getting rid of a frivolous woman, who was so clever moving her hands around the arch of his money and more "generous" than a crazy heir wasting his rich inheritance. And to compensate it he indulged in drinking, looking for the fundamental depression it brings to the drinker and the oblivion of misfortunes in front of the public gossip. And to be freer to do it, he exiled himself to New York and came to the Bowery, with the intention of proving his decision was formal and definitive to those who were following his itinerary. He spent some time among the drunkards to make sure to the same guys who were observing him that he really meant it and, when he wanted to say bye to the new colleagues and to the habit which he had practiced with them, he realized that it was already impossible for him. He then experienced some terror. He questioned himself if he had already developed the irreversible alcoholism. And to soften the rigors of the sudden shock, he decided to drink for another period until he could get rid of it, as he did with his wife.

One day in the morning he was lying in the angle made by the surface of the sidewalk and the wall of the façade of the bar *The world is mad*. With other three elements in his same position and around himself as they were protecting him from being trampled by the absent minded passersby and in order to stop his bad intentions of abandoning the Association of the Drunkards, which he now and then manifested and they were feeling it deplorable. Deplorable because they considered him element with a wonderful easiment to get the row material and of his prodigality to share it with them and even with the passersby. They recognized in him the Christian distinction in the middle of the deep sinking in the worst of the vices, which distinctive Christian virtue makes you to think in the other before you do in your own beast. Suddenly the man removed from his eyes a mop of hair, dusty with the urban pollution, and looked to the street, as a sleeping mastiff which wants to smell an intruder who just altered it with his smell. He jump to the air in an unreal manner, it's to say getting upwards in the horizontal position of the body, as he was pierced by a dagger in his hear.

"Mary!" he cried at the same time, as a shipwrecked person who claims for a board of salvation.

Everybody around him was awakened, lost and not knowing where to look.

"Mary!" Audrey shouted again, with a hoarseness which had a connotation of years of being waiting, with desperation and awful frustration.

It was a car which stopped near the sidewalk, driven by an older lady and a younger one, who wore an elegant skirt, got out of the car and shut her camera upon the ones lying in the sidewalk.

Audrey shouted louder and neither of the ladies was listening to him, because they were absorbed by the action of taking the photo. And they were not hearing him because of the trepidation of the traffic, which was louder and much more bothersome than the screams of Audrey. They neither heard or noticed him and took off because the scandal of the bullhorns behind them was noisier than his shouts. They took off and in the light of the corner they turned right.

Meanwhile Audrey got to stand up and ran the middle of the street to keep shouting and moving his arms in order that he could be seen by the ladies by the rear mirror. He was desperate for the loss of his former lover that could last again several years, or until death presented in the sinking into the ugly vice. To be ran over by a young driver who immediately speeded away, even not observing the red light in the corner. A pool of blood was being formed around the smashed body of Audrey.

The three drunkards who were lying around him in the sidewalk have noticed the accident and looked bewildered to the dead body, kneeled down beside him and with their hands in the asphalt. It could seem that they were praying for the soul of the dead one. May others of the association of the drunkards came to enlarge the group and with the intention that de running cars be careful not to hurt again anybody. After a reverent silence, one of them wets the top of his finger in the blood; he tastes it, esoteric, obscure and sad.

"Johnnie Walker!" he diagnoses, so persuaded.

"No!" counter affirms another, after tasting the blood in the same way. "It is Screwdriver!"

Another does the same. Tastes it, thinks for a moment, and rectifies moving his head.

"It's Bloody Mary, all right!", he makes known to them, in order that they understand they are wrong.

# The shadow of the skyscraper

During the month of March the polar north winds stopped sending its frigid gusts to the avenues of New York City. Those gusts were freezing the flashing signs which announce fishing tools, with water motifs. A premature warmer than usual wind defrosted this kind of signs and the citizens who circulated under the high building felt some anguish without any obstacle in the ground triggering it. In this situation they were turning their heads up to avoid getting in their bodies the smell of the rotten row fish. A unisex passerby, long hair with a lonely earring in the left ear, wearing fashion Texans, of neutral color and indefinite fitness, assured the walkers in the sidewalk that he got the impact of a rotten skeleton of a fish in his nape. Immediately a doctor, expert in dirty bruises, joined him saying that he got the same impact in his skull and a nursing man who was looking from a window of a clinic across the street and was terrified by the rain of the infinity of dirty particles falling upon people, which he could touch with his hand from there. The three of them went beyond this, announcing a possible invasion by air of lethal particles, with no precedents in the epidemic history of the City.

After that a series of strange deaths were happening which did not match with the medical previsions which to that moment had been typical in hospitals and other health centers. And these deaths were happening as well in a psychiatrist hospital or in the staircases of the subway, in the tub of the bathroom or in the window of the garden. With the common denominator of the formal suicide, having the victim all his senses awaken. The situation caused a mishap in the laboratories because the biologists organized ambitious culture mediums by means of the most atypical juices segregated by the terminal patients of that decease with no syndrome, to end by finding an odorless, colorless magma, chemically primary and totally empty of germs. "I suspect that we have here a parasite-bacteria complex with a death capacity so voracious that, once it has fed up of the habitat of the victim, the millions of the individuals devour each other until they eliminate themselves totally", commented, with a sad discouragement, Dr. Percy Cohen, chief of the Immunology Department of a prestigious hospital, in Borough Park.

Though this audacious appreciation, with more contains of impotence than of clinical penetration, was overcome by the opinion of other doctors in the metropolitan area who, with different formulations, not exempt of rhetorical itch, coincided in the suspicion that the epidemic could be a sprout of the virus of the black plague, slept during a whole millennium to awake when a so banal detail as the hypothetical corruption of a commercial sign is. At least this theory infused solemnity and historic sense to the problem and all the physicians felt the obligation of looking at it with seriousness and momentousness.

And the citizens did as well; after that joined declaration of the experts, a psychosis of menace of death spread all over the city of New York. Civic phenomenon which was reinforced by several preachers who, as those in the *La Peste,* of Albert Camus, when that also strange massive death of the rats made pressure upon the minds of the faithful with the idea of God's anger because of the sins of religious coldness and spiritual indifference, the kind of postmodern sins which push humanity to the end of the world. Great punishments and aberrant dislikes had to be expected from that deicide situation as in the middle age and in the occasions of the danger of contamination from that black plague, European fathers and mothers abandoned their infected children and grandparents to their final luck, under the irreducible criteria of preserving their own lives. The men were falling down as the dry leaves do in the autumn season, which was diluting in the air a color of death which could be touch by the hand.

Nevertheless the statistics were indifferent to that community mishap and they were getting loaded of frightful cyphers of deceases. The funeral parlors were full of corpses, but without making it public preventing the alarm of the citizens. The faces of their managers looked so somber to the living ones who came to arrange for a space for a beloved one dead, but intimately were happy because of the unusual amounts of bills for their arcs, only registered in the occasion of big plagues like this. So they were forced to fix very strict time tables for the deceased to wait to be religiously expedited, or to get lay attendance.

In this desperate situation, the Mayor Delaney send a message to the Federal Government reporting the helpless disorder that was finishing with the City of New York after having exhausted all the resources of the science and of the most advanced medicine against a public sickness that was killing so many citizens without defining itself to be attacked properly and with effectiveness. "Get ready to combat an enemy that kills and then manages to do as it does not exist", the Major pointed out. "It seems that it kills more, not because its virus, but because of the psychopathy that itself has spread among the citizens", the Major added downcast by a feeling of impotence which was very clear through the long of the note.

Washington read that note with extreme seriousness. Somebody in the White House controlled himself in front of the dark pessimism expressed by the leader of the Great Apple, because the plague was not whipping the Capital. But some of the closest councilors to the President did not wait to express their suspicion could be related to the lethal force of some secret arm invented by the enemy in the cold war and in the event that this was confirmed in the near future and in the reality, it could constitute one of the impediments more difficult to overcome for the Country since the problem of the Castro's missiles in Cuba. In front of this uncertain and so dangerous perspective, Mr. President played the most transcendental and save option, sending a note, written straight by his hand, ordering that, if all the scientific and epidemic resources were exhausted, they had to consult the most credited empiric healers in the street, who in the underground were practicing cures in cases of the desperate deceases, by means of antipodes herbs and of recondite dirty remedies. "But be careful", Mr. President insisted, "that the case does not reach to the ears of the chanceries of the other free countries of Occident ".

This kind of a top federal secret, though not issued by the Pentagon, the most sophisticated means were used, of human order as well as the technic order, by the city, federal and state policemen. And well instructed with a series of not clear data about how to locate the empiric healer, or the empiric lady, who might know the most unknown focuses of infection situated in the lowest crevices in the lowest infrastructure of the City, for example the underground conducts of the cancelled subway or the septic wells of the former and old Amsterdam, or the conducts of the obsolete web of the sewers of the XIX century.

All these data, by an obscure law of the instinct of conservation and by the suggestion of a good compensation, brought the officers to think of a ninety years old lady who lived in the street, whom they were used to see her leaned to the wall, close to the door of the Bowery Bank, in Forty Second Street and Lexington Ave., in Manhattan. Several times she leaned to the wall of the Bowery and some others to the wall of Chase Manhattan Bank. It seemed that the elderly woman was in this particular conduct to be seen by the passerby citizens, her body bend to the ground to refuse the almonds which the clients of the banks were offering her. She leaned to the walls by her ass and bending her thorax until forming an angle of 45 with her limbs. She never was talking to anybody, neither was looking at a single citizen, she appeared in the place at the sunrise and was out of the street at the first dusk of the evening not leaving any trace of herself. Many looked at her to define her nationality, but no one succeeded to do it, because her face was an enigma, wide as it seemed to be, but dry by her age and worm-eaten by the weather, which the same could suggest a Mongol origin as well as Korean, or Hawaiian, or Eskimo, or even Gipsy. But knowing her origins was not so important, since the officers were looking for her because many were saying that the old lady cured the aids of a nuts descendant of the Rothschild by means of her so secret medicines and being so indifferent about the fabulous sums of dollars given to her by the chief of the family to get from her the secret of that medicine. Her own life was a secret of empiricism and an anomalous case of longevity, which had no other explanation than the hidden capacities of the old lady.

But the officers were so much disappointed after the intense research to find her and never seeing her in any of the habitual daily places and wasted three days having a couple of them waiting her in those places. The chief policeman blamed them in a loud voice for their failure, out of the nervousness result of the fiasco.

"Either she is dead, or she is in some hospital being sick", concluded the corporals of the squads of research. And they dictated severe orders of organizing an intensive search in the urban hospitals and in its outskirts. Nobody knew what her name was and for this reason it was not convenient to go to inquire for her in the reception offices of the different centers, and so they were forced to look chamber by chamber, bed by bed, what was done in a notorious nervousness from the part of the doctors and the nurses and a bunch of scares of the patients and specially of those of dirty conscience, who really were battled enough by the voices of condemnation of the wrongdoings of all their lives.

Finally, the old lady was discovered by a Bowery depositor who was leaving the operating room upon a mat after undergoing a heart transplant in Brooklyn General Hospital. He identified her in spite of the torpors of the drowsiness, by the strait angle formed by the two halves of her body waiting upon another mat, in the waiting corridor. The woman was a patient in the hospital, bewildered by the excellent result of a liver transplant done in her neighbor in the room, she was fleeing from the nurses and was waiting for the good moment to slide into the operation room to watch the marvels the surgeons were performing in there by means of those unknown cures to her and to practice in the long period of life she was still promising to herself. She was waiting in that mat burning by fever, being one of its deliriums to penetrate the essence of the miracles never dreamed by her before in the long series of impossible cures of any kind she practiced.

Returned immediately to her room, the secret team of City doctors asked her to reveal to them what urban phenomenon –a black cloud, a commercial smock column, a funerary Cadillac, a camouflaged Sicilian gangster– was causing the plague which was cutting down so many citizens lives.

Notwithstanding been bothered, the old lady was generous to pay attention to them and talking to them. She simply said that the cause of so many deaths was the shadow in shape of a coffin of that high building in Forty Second Street between the Bowery and Chase Manhattan Bank, the skyscraper of Mining and Petroleum

Research Ltd. That shadow is ill-fated for the citizen and is the cause of this public plague which has no virus or medical history because she lived in the street counteracting the lives of her fellow citizens, standing always between those two banks counter acting the lethal effect of that shadow to protect them.

"It is the punishment of a jealous genius, angry for the cleaning of the universe that the scientist of the world are trying to do because of the warming of the planet and he concentrates in that shadow all the curse of the world air pollution which that crude enterprise and the similar ones spread all over the cosmos", the elderly added, making strange gestures with her arms and hands, upon her bed, cut by a death rattle.

Once this report got to the ears of the Major Delaney, he reacted beating the table with his fist, angry because he had sent a team of useless ambassadors who had been unable to ask the lady which could the right medicine to finish with the horrible decease in the air of the City.

Consequently he, himself in person, rushed to Brooklyn General Hospital in a very fast move to beat by legs the imminent danger of death for the citizens. He took with him two young ladies secretaries who were absorbed by their computers, in the Major's office, ordering them to take a carpet with several blank papers in order that between them two no small portion of a message given by the agonizing old lady could be written down.

The old lady opened with difficulty her eyes in front of the first authority of the City and did not show any anger for being bothered in her painful last moment. To the question of the Mayor asking what could be done to finish with the lethal effects of the shadow of that building shaped like a coffin, her face was illumined as it reflected the unknown happiness she was already experiencing in some known dimension and answered, making an effort:

"It has to be transplanted!"

And she delivered her soul to the Creator of the Universe.

# The flight of the drunkard

The manager of the prestigious firm Venetian Real State Corp. was an incorrigible drinker. Being so talented, recognized by the high finances of the Country, he had taken two leading enterprises in the field of the crude for energy from economic bankruptcy, The Petroleum and Gas Northfolk Ltd. and the Overseas Fuel Researcher Co., and he pushed them ahead and upwards in an splendid future of income. And at the end they both sacked him because, once their problems were solved with so brilliant action, he was keeping them in danger of a bankruptcy because he indulged too much in drinking and getting drunk every day more, what was degrading him mentally and nullifying the abilities of his genius.

"Yes, it is good for him that the enterprises dismiss him, once he has recuperated them, because he needs the challenge of the shipwreck and the vertigo that carries the menace of the disaster in whatever he is doing" his wife was explaining to the representatives of the New York Chamber of Commerce. "He drinks always but mainly when he sees in front of him a huge problem to be resolved because then, in the drunkenness situation, he conceives his genial solutions, the danger of sinking keeps him alert I challenges him, it touches his balls. But when everything goes easy, as upon wheels, he bores and falls in the cliff of human and professional irresponsibility –let alone in marital irresponsibility".

The ones from the Chamber of Commerce looked at one another consternated. The unusual case was impacting them so much, that they did not have anything to argue or to question about it. Everybody was internally sad for that privileged mind degraded by the worse of the destructing vices, when it could be a true asset for the most outstanding City finances and for all over the world. But they persisted in not having words for the case.

"As a drinker he is incorrigible, but if he did not drink, he would not be the genius he is", the woman added, in order that they did not make illusions and could verify the cruel deadlock in which she was placed as a lover and as a wife.

And since she saw them more consternated and speechless, none of them daring to look straight at her, because of the sexual problems included in the case, she kept saying:

"It is really convenient that you make very clear his condition when he is in dire crisis. He is always joyful, in that situation he sees everything pink color and he would never admit a personal defeat, but always he is triumphant in the thirst for the risk and even for the occasion of the heroic death. I can tell you that then the anxiety to experience known sensations is loosen in him and he tries to plunder the pleasures hidden in the intricate substance of the most unusual and unexplored risks in life.

Those from the Chamber of Commerce exit really disappointed from the talk with the lady. They did not know what to think about it, since they were getting away almost in the darkness because of the vertigo felt in their heads. They were sorry for

the loss of a citizen like this who, because of vulgar miseries, he
was missing to become a glory of the City, most possibly with a
planetary irradiation. All of them conceived it darkly, painfully,
but the youngest of the group did manifest that from time to time
it was convenient to bring some multinationals in the City to the
verge of bankruptcy in order that the individual in question could
exert his capacities to save what nobody else could redeem from
failure. "This thing will make its impact in the world!" he added
feeling proud because he had been the only to dare saying it.

All of them expressed a lot of recommendations to the delegate
from Venetian Real State Corporation to that assembly. "Keep him
from the excess in drinking as long as you can, because your relief
will not delay appearing", they recommended him, seeing his eyes
sparkling for the joy of his enterprise restored by that individual
to a normal and prosperous functioning.

Though the technic counsel of Venetian had not attended
that reunion, and so they had not listened to the lady manifesting
so many omens of ambiguous perspective. The whole of the
shareholders checked some unusual income and, as a lonely voice,
they decreed that it was absolutely indispensable to go ahead with
that ascendant line. With a young and pretty secretary to take care
of him and watch him, the individual can survive for a long period
and do good to the enterprise and bring it up to a level of income
that we cannot jeopardize" all agreed in unison.

The secretary with such characteristics was assigned to him and
good success proved that the idea could not be happier and more
opportune. The incorrigible and the young lady played a loving
game of hiding and finding, the exiting game of the espionage and
of the evilness of making himself absent –always adorned with
the simulation of mother nature's impositions– to look for the
protection behind a door in the corridor to take several sips from
a Chivas Regal bottle, kept in some secret hiding place, to enjoy
the company of some colleague, residing in the same skyscraper.

In this aspect the incorrigible matched with the manager of Florida Land Development Enterprise, with whom he made frequent conspiracies inside the complex of the building, under the pretext of some reunion or of other meetings of professional character. This colleague became the most serious handicap to the diligent secretary.

She was alarmed by the fact that her watched friend became addicted so easy to that colleague, without using any dirty trick to subdue him. That friend of his was a drug, he was another dimensions of the alcohol, a plus intoxication upon the basic intoxication. One day his watched one left the office for an unusual period of time and this alarmed her more than in some other occasions. To the extent that she decided to get out of the office to go in search of the fugitive in order to find him, not paying any attention to his lies and excuses, even getting in some places not so convenient for a young lady to visit.

When she was walking in a corridor at the bottom of which there was an open window to the avenue, she saw a fast shadow crossing it up-down. She almost fainted, she started perspiring, coldly, and her limbs were failing like not supporting her anymore.

Well, this fact deserves been stretched, the research of its process and the meaning of that shadow. The two friends, and drinkers, coincided in the foyer of the floor where the one from Florida had his office, looking for a cup of coffee, making at the same time some legs exercise. Once in their element, they missed something more perverse than what they had and the friend rushed to his office and came back with two bottles of Johnny Walker Black Label, not yet open. They celebrated to be alone and far away from the eyes always so alert of the secretaries. They turned that little bit of freedom into a bliss. The two bottles were empty in an unreal period of time.

When they were thinking to go back to their offices, somebody got out of the elevator and this stayed for a short while quiet and empty in front of them. They both got in under an indefinite idea about where they were going to. But that instrument was open and soaking them and could do nothing against it.

"Where are you going?" the friend asked the other, ready to push the button.

"To Cuba!" answered the other, under the impulse of what the numerous skyjackers of commercial airplanes were used to answer at that time.

They both laughed the joke with strength and shacking, which had their origin in the stomach region. The buttons of the elevator were pushed at random. The elevator took them to the roof of the building.

They were startled at sunlight that irradiated up there, up in a building of eighty floors. They threw their hats to the air and they moved to the center to absorb the sun and the fresh air. They could see the top of the main buildings of the City and this particular excited them as they were discovering them for the first time. They rushed to rival calling the buildings by their names to beat each other; the Empire State Building, The Twins, the Grand Central, that other one belongs to Chrysler Corporation! They rushed together to the balustrade of the roof and became startled in front of the panorama offered by the jungle of the incredible bulks of the City. They were vibrating out of emotion, they felt transported to an imaginary and happy paradise, the world and its joys were splendid, they were feeling it out of question by the effluviums of their stomachs toward their hearts. The bottom of the avenue was down there in an infinite distance, like something unreal, the cars were circulating there as quite vivid insects, men were moving down there as insignificant ants. But to be true, that empty space was sucking them, it exerted a strong attraction because of the thirst to explore known sensations and to sack their internal joy.

"Bestial!" the friend exclaimed, drunk of that deep majesty and its abstract attraction, yet pressing attraction.

"Brutal!" confirmed the one from Venetian. "It has to be brutal to possess this space with the open arms like a huge pray bird!"

"It has to be bestial let your person go upon this empty space!" insisted, out of his senses the one from Florida. "Do you imagine what has to be felt flying down there?" the one from Florida asked pushing him in the ribs.

"It has to be fantastic! It has to be absolutely fancy!"

"Try it! Fly down there, it has to be bestial!" the friend insisted on him.

The one from Venetian was getting up the balustrade and was standing there for a moment. He was raving, sending deep breaths to the empty space down his feet.

"When you are flying, let me know how it feels, please!" his friend begged him. "You'll experience an orgasm of triumph unique over all the human kind of this planet!" I am the next, after you!"

The one from Venetian threw himself to the empty space.

And when he was around the twentieth story of that building, he turned around up to his friend and shouted to him:

"So far, so good!"

# The Guernica Painting
# against Saint Patrick's

*I*ñaki Olavarria worked as an usher in the Olympic Tower. This Tower stands up in Fifth Avenue and Fiftieth Street, just in front of the pathetically silent Rockefeller Center. This detail could be meaningless, but it was not because of the secret rivalry existing between the traditional Gothic spires of the bell towers on Saint Patrick Cathedral and the postmodern sparkling of the glasses of the structure of the Olympic Tower. The bulk of the Cathedral across the street becomes so low, insignificant and without capacity to be reverenced from the arrogant neighbor.

The location of the Tower, with its forty stories of altitude, exactly besides the sacred building, hurt Iñaki's sensitivity, it had been a dire pain to his eyes in the first time he visited the section. He could do no more about it, that fact seemed to him an awful idea of an evil urban plan. The owners and the inmates of the Tower had to be a kind of iconoclasts and the busyness going on in there necessarily had to be dirty, it's to say, brewed according to the parameters of the Mafia and to the obscure interests of the most without God lobbies of the world.

Iñaki came from a Christian family of Donostia, Euzkadi, and he was keeping good religious feelings, though he was not the most faithful in the external practices, but rather allergic to the traditional methods of practicing faith. He was a member of the underground organization ETA and was fulfilling several years of a voluntary exile in the most vital metropolis of the *laisser faire* in the world, while the Spanish police was losing his memory, after having implied him in a crime he never committed. In spite of the fact that he agreed with everything that implied fight to free Euzkadi from the unjust power that prevented it from been free and sovereign, as every nation in the world has the natural right to it. "They are the ones who promote war!" was his answer to the one who questioned him about his Country. "To subdue a nation which is born to be free, and wants to be free, is violence and a crime against humanity", was his political motto, visceral and ideological. "Euzkadi is the victim of a state terrorism for centuries", he added to it.

When he realized that the enterprise which promised him a job had to be around that place, Iñaki was bitterly disappointed. When he was arriving there walking Fifth Avenue up and was already in the corner of Forty Five Street, he felt a contrariety in his heart as he was approaching the bulk that he previously knew and was afraid that it could be the destination of his new job. And it was right it! He had to make an effort to get in and ask for the chief receptionist. He needed to take the job, if he wanted to make a living and establish the basis for a better life, from where he could be able to look at human stupidity.

So he started working as an usher in the Olympic Tower. Between the short periods left in between the different reception of personal he was performing, and while he was accompanying some in the premises, was glancing the cathedral through the wide glasses and was amazed of the architectural details he was discovering. When he was getting to the higher stories, he was disappointed having to lower his eyes to see the old pinnacles down there, at the derisory altitude in what they were left by the commercial, technical highness of the Olympic Tower. He imagined that his feet were "committing a horrible sacrilege", according to the nomenclature infused so many times by his grandmother when he was a little boy and she taught him to conceive a respect for the sacred buildings and their contents. "Really, it was an unforgivable irreverence and an ugly note given by this Country to the thousands and thousands of visitors to this artistic jewel".

The injury had a boomerang effect upon his religious feelings. Moved by a sentiment of amends, which he did not even noticed, he was getting frequently into the cathedral and was fascinated looking at the beautiful effects of the architecture and the sculpture, or seated for a while to pay a reflexive tribute to the divinity, as he understood it, or he amused himself contemplating the variegated aspect offered by the cosmopolitan crowds visiting the temple, keeping always his ears ready to get the whispering in Euzkera, what now and then happens over there.

One day, on leaving the work at dusk, he saw an unusual crowd in front of the cathedral. The Latin accents were heard everywhere. He asked somebody what was all about and three or four people answered him at unison that it was the celebration of the Virgin of Guadalupe, *Patrona de la Hispanidad,* "Patroness of the Spanish World". He decided to see how the easy going of the Spanish was combined with the Irish and Yankee rigidity of the general structure, both material and spiritual, of Saint Patrick's. The cathedral was jammed and painfully he found some empty space to stand up. Some celebrant was preaching with a hard Spaniard accent from the *Meseta central,* from the Castilian

Plateau: *La madre Patria la unidad española el destino común..
la falsa vision histórica de los nacionalismos el terrorismo asesino
y separatista...* (The Mother Country... the Spaniard unity... the
common destiny... the false historic vision of the nationalisms...
the assassin and separatist terrorism...) combined concepts with
fervor expressions of love to the Virgin Mary and of praise to her
title of Guadalupe as the *Capitana de las Españas.* (Captain of the
Españas).

The ambient in the sanctuary caused bitterness in the heart of
Iñaki. He repented being there. He started taking of, with much
difficulty among the so tied people and, before he got into the
vestibule, he could see the preacher standing in front of the micro
and in the altar cardinal O'Connors seated and wearing the purple
biretta. The chief representative of the Diocese of New York was
listening to words he did not understand and for which he would
not give a penny, in case he understood them. Iñaki considered
everything grotesque in there, of a bad taste and abusive upon the
mass of the used to admit the yoke they suffer upon and to keep
silent, and to the respect for the solemnity in church.

He got out escaping from the profanation of the cathedral,
worse profanation indeed than the one coming from the Olympic
Tower, worse because the responsible were favoring it by means of
a farce and ignoring the official hierarchy what they were exactly
presiding. He walked until Fifty Three Street toward his subway
station and, crossing in front of the Museum of Modern Art, he
experienced a vague desire to watch the Guernica painting. He
was presenting on it veracity, sincerity and free accusation of
crime in front of the falsifications of life. He jumped up the second
floor. He stood in front of the Picassos's painting; the agonizing
and strident swarming of the painting made him forget the anger
conceived in the cathedral... and conceive another anger.

It was in the rush hour and he found it clear of lookers in.
The torn members, flying in the air; the heads of the living bulls,

contracted by the sign of the extermination with hatred from
the part of the enemy; the arms and the limbs cut off; the claim
of craziness of a people suppressed because it wanted to be free
and not to be suppressed, appealed straight to his sacked soul.
There was a hidden reference to the human beast when it tries to
impose its will to the universe and does not stop it in front of the
destruction of the universe. He was spelled looking at that mosaic
of air-splitting screams, resounding in helpless cries, swelled with
infant groans, saturated of grandparent's silences. "The authors of
injustice have to be blown out from the face of the world, exactly as
it is done by this painting which displays the photogenic hatred to
my nation", he was proclaiming inwardly. The voice of the usher
of the museum telling him it was the time to close the building,
awoke him from his pain in the heart.

From that time he grew some apprehension toward Saint
Patrick's. The Guernika painting, yes, was being friendly
toward his wanted faith in the upsetting of humanity. Instead
of getting under the volt of the cathedral –which for him had
loosed the blessing palpation of a paternal hand– was visiting
the other Methodist church of Saint Thomas with its interior
sweet by a penumbra, at the corner of Fifth Avenue and Fifty
Three Street, half the way between the cathedral and the
Guernica painting.

The building, of pure Romanesque style, is a marvel, a true
miracle because of the place it occupies, so commercial and so
noisy, so cosmopolitan. Inside, its nudity establishes a utopic
silence and the most beaten souls by unavailable ideals or by
love fantasies that the enemy does not allow to be profiled come
here looking for light or for some consolation in their desperate
solitude in the middle of the turbulent City. In his first visits to
the place Iñaki could realize that all the present showed in their
attitudes that charisma of being familiar to the monastic character
of the place. A place where frivolous looks never happen. Neither

articulated salutations in whisperings ever happen. Where the just two, three lonely ones, follow their Stations of the Cross of memories in the stony corners or seated or kneeled down in the penitent pews. Little by little he learned to be at ease with the absence of a noisy worship, empty of praises, yet rich with that naked religion which looks for the truth of freedom in every creature, which in the long run ends in the Lord of Heaven.

Before a week elapsed in this spiritual fluctuation between the Guernica and Saint Patrick's, remembering the personal pain mysteries, when some of the most faithful to the place forgot about his contemplation under a basilisk capital that keeps its mouth open menacing to devour that one who may enter in without any intention of praying, said to him:

"I belong to the Sinn Féin" said in an approach equivalent to the disclosure of a long itinerary of synchrony with his thoughts.

Iñaki was so surprised that he had no words to answer him.

"So…" he only said before swallowing saliva which silenced him; crack, emitted his Adam nut in the neck. He felt gratefully undressed by the spontaneous guy.

Then the Nord-Irishmen opened his arm to point out to him the others contemplatives under different architectural artistic elements and four came to the appointment.

"This one is Giovanni Doudo, born in Ajaccio, cradle of the crazy Napoleon, who opposed the Jacobin French Government and fights for the freedom of his Country. He is a true and sincere Corsican. He is persecuted by the establishment.

Another young man had come and, in order not to interfere, he was waiting with his anxious eyes and a smile of affinity with the conversation.

"He is a Kurd" the Irishman introduced him, being this the not officially declared dean of the solidary group. "He does not speak English, yet he takes very active part in the dialogues. He keeps deep wounds in his soul because of the atrocities committed against his nation by the genocidal countries like Russia, Turkey and Iraq. He is persecuted by the establishment too.

Another quit the beating of the polluted sunlit from the avenue through one of the few windows of the place. He met the group after a spiritual impetus.

"I am René Poujada", he saluted the group, not observing any protocol. "I keep the spiritual wound caused by king Pere, the Catholic and I fled from Muret, not being able to listen to the words of indignation for the injustice of that war. Here I suffer and pray for the freedom of my Country, Occitan. But I also had to get out of there because I am persecuted by the French Government because I raised my voice against the official French Church historically opposed to the interests of my Country and because I was teaching the youth how to love and practice our mother language".

There was another penitent who accused malnutrition and a daily inhuman effort to extinguish bitter thoughts. He also came to the group, bringing in his face the shadow of the cloud secreted by his lonely condition.

"The establishment that persecutes all of you is Saint Patrick's. Because it is the oligarchy, the meeting point of the delegates of the artificial States" he poured over them, twisting his pupils to the spires of the cathedral of Saint Patrick's. "All of you are gone there looking for a solace and an understanding of your spiritual wound, while you have realized that it is a place sold to the powerful. And it has become inhospitable to you. And you went to the Guernica. And because the Guernica frightened you, you came here looking for the wisdom in between, to take refuge in the nakedness of the Romanesque. I beat you all been the first to come. The Romanesque will soon tell you that no way, that the Guernica is right: turning men into pieces, the carnage, it is to say, the revolution to do away with de despotic farce according to which the powerful have arranged the world against de destitute and disarmed".

And he returned to his place, not willing to listen to comments.

Iñaki got horrified in front of the iniquity of the world, as those visionaries were exposing it. So, then, all present there have underwent the same experiences he had endured, coarse, dark, without any hope.

"This is the first time I heard him talking physically…" the Irishman said about the one who talked last. "He defends that the only available resource for justice is the demolishing and cruel action against the powerful and despots States of Europe and Asia that keep their nations subdued to their rule and oppression, in spite that this action may be suicidal for the time being… I break my head trying to elucidate whether he is a Chechenyan, a Palestine, a Cypriot or a Kurd.

# The innocent who
# read a pupil

he little Christopher enjoyed a lot sliding down through the handrail of the balustrade beside the staircase that descends from the door of the building where he lived to the sidewalk. He slid in his womb to the stony top, smooth because the many times he was doing it; to get his hands whistle, after a spat he threw to the chiseled stone, was a triumph for him. The amusement was alienating him to the point of not paying any attention to the world that surrounded him or to the people getting up the staircase o getting down; his maximum joy was inviting some friend to it in order that he made competition with him in the other balustrade to see who was first to touch with his head the pylon at the end, near the sidewalk and was whistling more. It was so difficult for his mother to withdraw him from the amusement, calling him for dinner from the second floor window.

Some day at noon was playing alone his preferred game. He was anxious to have some rival, but none was coming and his mother had prohibited him to go to the neighboring houses looking for one. Nevertheless he discovered one, or at least a companion, on getting down to that pylon where he saw the eyes of a little dog, seated in the sidewalk, which was looking at him with a deep sadness.

There was something unusual in the eyes of that pet! He was looking at him with great sadness, all right, but also begging some help from him in its affable and timid attitude. Christopher was emotionally moved by that look and got down the balustrade and went to caress the poor little one, sliding his hand on its head and the abundant and clean hair of its back. Seeing how the pet was enjoying his caresses but not changing the cloud of sadness that covered his eyes, he took it in his arms and pressed it to his chest; the easy beast enjoyed the hug with a feeble and like done far away howl, which reinforced the sense of desolation for Christopher, the sense of missing something loved and lost, the sense of missing a caress like the one it was getting by himself. In that very moment his mother called him for lunch, through that window.

The boy left the dog in the ground and said bye to it with a forcible obedience to his mother. The little beast made a short, painful howl and followed him with his sight while was jumping the grades of the staircase and disappeared up home. Christopher was getting up to the second floor taking impressed in his eyes the profile of something that could be some human face… under a tear upon the pupil of the dog. The soul of the young man was bewildered about that indefinite profile. He was unable to define what it meant, but he had for granted that it had much to do with the sadness of the pet.

It was on a Saturday afternoon and he did not have to go to school. As soon as he had eaten with the family, he escaped from the table and got down to the street to meet his friend; he had reserved a sandwich in his pocket, from those prepared by his mother for the lunch, most possibly with the acquiescence not expressed of the mother, since she was always encouraging her children to be compassionate to the most helpless creature. Once in the sidewalk, Christopher looked around, first nearby, and then to the environment in order to see where the good friend was, and he was devastated not seen it in any place around. "They stole it from me!" he exclaimed, desolate.

And he decided to obey the rule of his mother permitting him to play only on the side walk around the whole block. He walked in it with the sandwich in his hand and shortly before the second corner he saw some eyes which were looking at him from behind some garbage containers. It was his friend; which approached him wagging just a little bit its tail, its pupils up looking at him, in which still was that tear upon the profile of something, Christopher did not exactly what it was. He placed the sandwich in the ground and invited the little one to go ahead. The dog smelled it, rather indifferent, and did not bite it, wagging a little bit more the tail in order that he could see it was grateful about it.

"It is not a matter of hunger, young man, because I keep this dog well nourished" a lady who was ready to jump that staircase said to him. "This pet is around here for a couple of weeks, lost; surely somebody has to be searching it".

Christopher took it again in his arms and brought it in front of his house. He was seeing his friend so downcast and desolate that he made the resolution to do whatever he could to find his owner and return the happiness to it. He placed it in his lap and, caressing it, he stood there expecting that somebody was passing by and could claim it as his propriety. But before was his mother who appeared in the door of the building and showed herself displeased with that excessive care for the unknown pet.

"Let this dog go in order it can return home or somebody takes it" the mother ordered him, very strictly. "Now you have to accompany me to buy in the supermarket, because I cannot do it alone".

The boy let the dog go free. He liked going shopping with his mother, but that day he did not like it, because he had to abandon his friend to his sad situation. Anyway he shut up and went with his mother to the supermarket.

The both of them in a Nova driven by his mother went to the *The Best Buy Supermarket,* at a distance more or less of ten blocks from home and at the limits of Harlem. Christopher enjoyed the magic of getting a car for the buy with a piece of metal inserted in the slot, in the parking lot and drive it inward the large store. He was the official wheel man; from his place he said advises to his mother about what was best to buy and frequently he ordered her very strictly.

Absorbed by this routine, suddenly his eye was pierced by some vision. Highly startled, he left the car abandoned in the corridor and went to look through another. He was scrutinizing a lady who just got in there and now she was checking some product from the shelves she held in her hand. He withdrew from that position before she could discover him looking so intensely at her. He suffered a beating in the heart. He waited a moment and he left his hiding place and walked toward that lady to see her face straight looking toward him.

Then he went to his mother and told her: "Mother, let's go home right now to get that little dog!" said to her breathing strongly, truthful.

"My goodness! My son! What's the need for this now?" his mother moderated him.

"Let's go home right now!" he insisted with authority, trusting the good endeavor of the mother.

She knew her child. She thought that something wordy of paying attention to his request was going on. She brought the buying car have full with several items to a corner where it could not be in the way of anybody. Then she and the child walked to the car in the parking lot and drove speeding as much as she could to the front of their building. The infant got out of the car immediately and came back to it bringing the little dog in his arms; he had found it nearby those containers under the volt of the staircase; the little beast looked cheerful and at ease in the chest of the boy feeling by instinct something special in the air.

The mother was not at ease with what was going on, she was afraid of some legal complication, a lost dog... an unknown owner... ay unexpected trouble.

"Son, I am not sure that you are correct getting involved in this dangerous matter... Don't get involved, taking care of this lost dog, think that some bad owner could create legal problems to get advantage of your good will..." she was preventing his child.

"Mother, don't be afraid. I know everything so well!" he insisted, trying to comfort his mother, pressing the pet against his chest.

As soon as they got into the supermarket, the dog smelled the air and jumped to the ground form Christopher's arms. It touched the ground and ran to one of those corridors with shelves in each side. Mother and child ran also to it to see what was coming up next, and they saw the dog jumping to the arms of that same lady Christopher had scrutinized a while ago, heaving a howl of joy and love, and also of reencounter. The lady hugged it exhaling another howl even more inenarrable of love and happiness, even more zoological, kissing the dog in the top of its snout. After some time of such effusions, the lady place the dog with tenderness in her buying car upon the products, and kept looking at the shelves, not caring about who brought her dog in or how it got in there. Just leaving a corridor and starting in another, with her eyes captive of her little idol looking at her while leaking its lips and wagging its tail furiously, beating with it the products beneath, in the car.

"And how have you done, my son, to know that she was the owner of this lost dog?" the mother was questioning the son, during their return home.

And the son had no words to explain to his mother what had happened in the whole matter.

# Platonic Love

*J*oe Rabbit was the lonely walker on the paths built upon solid grounds in the marshes of Jamaica Bay. It's good that we underline the Importance of that bird sanctuary within the metropolitan area of New York City. Joe uses to be there at the middle of the afternoon and walks around concentrated in his thoughts, loaded with a tripod, with the limbs of the instrument kept ahead of his body in order that they cannot bother walking, and with a black bag where he carries the items for the photography. Which he does from a distance and closer, yet always wise, scientific, absolutely looking for a rare subject and never for a trifle. He cuts the chilly air in winter time with his pointed nose, so much like the one of a fakir, and wearing a hat made off a black cloth with a red band and a blue tassel dancing in the top, which hardly covers the farinaceous white color of his boldness, making an image wordy to be standing in the wax museum of the City, belonging to the most illustrious paranoiacs in the Great Apple area. His so white skin color is due to the anemia caused by a diet submitted to the limitations imposed by the amnesia and the concentration in some persistent mania; the guy is really crude wax for an inanimate museum.

Joe has an incredible capacity to get high in the cleanest sphere of darkness, to get into the most refulgent optimism or to sink in the most deep and abyssal depression with no exit. He is crazy about the migrant birds and the exotic samples which just now and then stop in the marshes. The sign of his craziness is decided by the rare bird visiting the marshes that afternoon to rest for a while, may be a not classified coming from the most known corner of the planet, or even the stupidity of the human beast corrupting the quietness of the silence which he demands to be observed by anybody upon his piece of a paradise.

This latest aspect of his personality is the hidden cause of the anthropophagy that Joe breathes. One needs to be very careful just to salute him: today he shakes your hand and makes to you brilliant explanations about his last findings of rare birds, tomorrow he rejects your salutation and snaps a grunt to your face, walking away from you as a mommy or a caryatide come down from a sarcophagus. And the he gets lost, as a rare beast himself to be studied, going to where his pure animal instinct guides him. He looks for a shelter among the bushes, which the only thing that grows in this terrain beaten by the northern frigid gales, on winter time, and parched by the coarse sunshine on summer time. When he is alone and quiet uses to look around and faraway with his binoculars, as he had the key of the Universe closed in them.

But the intensity of this delight does not last long. Soon you see him getting up and raise his fist to the space as the one who puts a bomb in it to turn it into pieces. The cause is a jumbo. Nearby, in the running ways for landing in Kennedy airport, heating the motors and making noise to make the environment tremble, there is a jumbo ready to take off. And at the moment the flying monster flies upon him, he spats on it with an incredible devastation and a true intention of getting it to destroy it. Seen his saliva scattered by the wind, he gets furious to an incredible extent, which emanation alarms more than one passerby.

One afternoon I found him hiding behind a bush in a kind of a garden, like an oasis in the park, looking through the leaves with his naked eyes, his face radiant because he was enjoying a series of recondite delights.

"Watch it!" he said on hearing the noise of my feet, putting his finger in front of his lips.

He did not recognize me. He was muttering not looking at me; he was blaming the human beast, in general. He was watching a hunchbacked bird, similar to the craven or to the crow, of a black color, but with a tint of vinegar, like the dry bark of the maple tree and with more affable traces than those of the black predator of the space and of the dirty soil, which was pecking the grass nearby an open space, in the middle of a weedy vegetation.

The bird was really a rare species. I wonder how it could stand these eyes of Joe so inflamed, like the ones of a spelled wild animal. It was distinguished by aristocratic presence, it accused a vague conscience of its category as a bird, it raised its leg with elegance, it was shacking its wings with a style, its hump suited it like the one of a usurer of the New York high life.

Then Joe approached me. Slowly. Not making any noise, not losing from his sight the object of his spell.

"It is the only one remaining in the planet of his kind!" he snapped to me, grinding his teeth, surely alluding to an infamous liquidation of the species. "It could be the only one in any galaxy!" he added shaking, twitching. "It belongs to… (I cannot remember what he said in Latin, with a heavy English accent which anyway made it unintelligible; I am useless even to understand things wrongly pronounced in a strange language!).

What happened the following days was a matter of witches. The bird and the bird watcher had verified an incredible approach, absolutely familiar and relaxed. The spiritual communication was more than obvious. Lying on his belly on the grass, the naturalist scrutinized the sample standing jut a foot away of his nose, with the internal projection of the most avid sweetheart. He was following it among the brush wood, he spied in short distance its propagandistic pose, getting it with avarice into the photo camera. It seemed like they were talking, silence was pouring from one to the other pushed and attracted by a mysterious osmosis. I have seen the birds distrustful and elusive all over the world. Plus, I have seen them rapacious. That one had to be a female, by the way it flirted, the way it was listening to the flowers Joe was saying to her, by the style she was "posing" in front of the camera when Joe was ready to shoot her. It was the situation of Adam and Eve in the Earthy Paradise, afterwards lost so sadly.

Until in one of those afternoons, walking in the pathways, absent minded, enjoying the breeze from the ocean and the lukewarm sun I discovered a scene among the brushwood. I stopped… I scrubbed my eyes, I moved back a couple of steps. A frigid stream went down my spinal. Several feathers, a fire, a pan, where something was hissing… Good heavens!

"Joe, what are you doing? What, Joe…? What…? I don't want to believe that…!"

His face was that of a spirited man. Anybody could say that his blood was boiling in cold. He was seated on a stone, he was eating swallowing up. He was cleaning a leg of the bird spelled bound, while in the pan the rest of the body was hissing. The feathers on the ground belong, out of any doubt, to that rare bird, his friend. He was eating it and with a joyful satisfaction.

"It is the culminating moment of the true love!" he grumbled deafly. The only possible orgasm and a gratifying one" he snapped to me with a notorious, sinister air. "It was the only surviving from the general depredation of the human beast… The season of its migratory moment was approaching… To which hand would my beloved bird go to finish its unique and transcendental life? Oh, jealousy was breaking my heart!"

He got up, trembling, continuing to chew with delight. He snapped for the first time his burning eyes to mine, with his libs totally soiled with grease.

"Instead of finishing with a miserable death, it will live in me forever. Its hormones will join mine and they will pass to my children and to the children of my children until the umpteenth generation. I and my descendants will be the living tomb of a selective species, innocent victim of the number one predator in the cosmos, which is the human beast".

He concentrated again in his stomach sally. He forgot about me. He rejected his friend for so many years.

My upheaval persisted. I was not reacting in any aspect. I moved with my arms ahead of me like walking in the darkness, in spite that I was under a magnificent sunlight, fleeing away from a dazzled and dazzling world.

That afternoon I opened my eyes to the reality that this world is full of a dirty materialism, paunchy, vulgar and limitless predator. From that time the absurd, the aberrant and the macabre do not alter my blood, they get from me and absolutely cold reaction.

Since then I have not trusted at all platonic loves, ecologist precautions, mystic ecstasies, supernatural raptures and altruistic concerns…

(But, be careful, because the conviction observed by Joe chewing and cleaning the bones of the unfortunate bird was the final compensation for a long period of standing impious hunger!)

# The 666 number

The green color is emblematic of Ireland. And it is too the most exalting one of its country side. The Irish girls wear it in their skirts, on March 17, because it alludes to the greenness of their mother island, which is through all the year the "Emerald of the North Atlantic". But in that day even the sympathizers wear green color during the parade in honor of their Patron, Saint Patrick, which makes a sumptuous transformation of Fifth Avenue.

The Mayor Lindsay, in that uncertain 1973, suffering the restrictions of the energy crisis –which was threatening to crush the national economy because of the greedy speculation of the petroleum magnates of the wide world–, wanted to inject some optimism to the City inviting the Indians, who had been the first inhabitants of the island of Manhattan, to all events on the feast of Saint Patrick. In this way all the heads of the tribes and their councils who lived up State were invited to the feast, especially to the parade in the afternoon. They live in some nucleus of the country side, cornered there, put aside and suffering because of the robbery by the white man of the lands which belong to them and to which they, the Indians, have never renounced; in the most secondary lands they reside now, were "granted" by the Federal Government, called "Reservations".

The racket of the organization of the parade upon the roadway of Fifth Avenue and in front of the Central Park, bothered the Indians, so used to the silence and to the good accord which reigned upon their ancestral states, and they joined to make a cluster in the middle of the mess in order to avoid being pushed and beaten in order not to be dispersed. Eye of Lynx, head of the tribe of the Mohawks, a tall old man, thin, with a protruded nose and sunk eyes, black like the ones of the lynx, was the reference point around which all the Indians have to gather. Among them there was no one giving orders; the movements of the individuals were measured and minimal, they looked frequently to the old man and approached him, with the smoothness of the plant which bends to the light, and paid much attention to his face because it reflected the rules to be followed. But also read on it the emotions and opinions about whatever was happening in the parade to accept them with pleasure or with no pleasure. They are a race used to the restful silences and to the facial and intuitive communication, which on them are a sense of animal character, but telluric, unknown by the damaged generation by the influx of the white man.

Their group was walking behind the orchestra of City College, integrated by masculine and feminine musicians, of different statures and volumes, all of them wearing perfect uniforms of skirt and jacket, both of a green color like the heaven craped by the top of the Empire State Building and a crease from the upper chest to the shoes, flying according with the pace of the music. The Indians were peering through the musical instruments and were absorbed by the filigrees performed with sticks, hats, copes and the thighs of the majorettes, these ones being graceful, mischievous and attractive, who were rotating in front of the musicians turning their job so difficult. The Indians were grasping that play +with their inscrutable faces, stung by the rodent bugs of their manes and, it has to be said, with segments of sense reserved to the other factors in the sides of the Avenue and even farther, in the streets.

The sidewalks of Fifth Avenue were jammed with amazed and anxious people looking at the group of Indians, crowds with a connotation of a parenthesis, it's to say, with a curious and precarious look, being ready not to lose any other detail of the parade and expecting the principal event of the day. Those crowds were oppressing the soul of the chief of the tribes; one could read in his face that he considered them vulgar, prosaic and profane of the sacred place where so many generations of his ancestral had lived a life in intimate contact with Mother Nature. A tear hung for a moment from his eyelid and fell to the ground; tear which had more than one replay among the old men who surrounded him and who were keeping a tone with his temper. None of the group wanted to turn his eyes to the left not to meet the bulk of the Metropolitan Museum, because they knew that it is full of items from their past, among the many items belonging to the life of the tribes and because they were support of family life, of true loves, of feasts, of mourning, of costumes and of leisure. They were turning them to the vegetation that fills the Central Park, because that was giving to them the taste offered then by the ambient before the depredation done by the white civilization. They were filling their eyes with that green color of Mother Nature! They were crying their suppressed world, were protesting against their confinement and against the menace upon their survival as the original people, lord of the land, while accusing the authorities and the rapacious public filling the sidewalks.

And it happened that the vision of nature suddenly finished on stepping in Sixty Street. Exactly there the eyes of the Indians were surprised by the bulk of the Hotel Plaza; a building crowned with a petulant skylight, ornamented with draperies hung from the balconies, with a lot of carriages parked in the square, the horses of which were waiting, yoked and behaving with an skeptic and painful resignation, similar in all to themselves, the Indians. The squeezing that follow immediately and again in Fifth Avenue decided the sensation of stuffiness experimented by the heads of the tribes.

And another sudden shock waits for them on reaching the corner of Fifty Three Street. All they were pierced by punches of metal in a dirty way; attached to the wall under a porches formed by the columns of a skyscraper, just in front of the church of Saint Thomas, the number 666 was hanging, large like a damned cipher, poisonous with evil omens and blaspheme in front of the sanctity of the Romanesque style. The Indians could not avoid a gesture of panic. But also did it to protect their lives from the irradiation of that sign. The old patriarch muttered a prayer to Odem, the Second Spirit of God, mystery which makes his voice heard by the winds and communicates the breath of live to the world. And that builds the bridge between the ancestral believes and the practices of Sioux and the sacred book of the Christian Apocalypse. Foot of Deer, of the tribe of the Iroquois, and Nose of Fox, from the tribe of the Massapequa, answered his prayer in a loud voice in order to make stronger the exorcism. Though the public did not pay any attention to the number, some were passing by it running and almost scrubbing it with their front head –contumacious, filthy, infected as it was, and without realizing its presence. People were persistent on looking at the Indians, but nobody was able to notice any alteration in their insensitive, remote and colorless faces.

"This is the cypher of the name of the Beast!" the lanky patriarch muttered to every ear. And made it reach beyond any ear of the children of the tribes.

"It is the number of the Antichrist!" exhaled another of the old men, from de Montauks, spontaneous, not being able to moderate it.

"It is New York!" two more muttered, with exact emotional and psychic conditions.

"This building is the lair of the organized crime! Here, those who have eradicated us, prosper!" the lanky old man execrates.

**They keep a mute dialogue among themselves in a stiff and feverish circuit. All of them raised a fist against the cursed bulk of a building, an invisible fist. Because the Indian suffers, agonizes, but does not exhale a sigh, he does not move a hand or an eyelid in the sense of a complaint. The march of the group became more hazardous, more uncertain; they were getting away from that cursed cipher as fast as they could not to generate suspicions in the observers, yet with panic and conjuring the malefic influences by means of words of tribal exorcisms learned from the old heads and from the grandmothers closest to Odem, the Second Spirit of God.**

**But on passing between Saint Patrick and Atlas, who raises the globe of the world with his arms and muscles, all of them encouraged the colossus to complete his effort throwing it against the camouflaged iniquity circulating in front of him at his very feet. It is the iniquity which suppressed and suppresses now the people off the sacred land.**

**"A day will come when your own lying world will fall upon you, New York and will smash you!" still muttered the old patriarch to his followers, with a large tear sliding down his chick.**

**And then his word was explicit and powerful. The municipal authorities, who were parading just behind them, heard him too and experienced panic for the emotional hermetism of the group of Indians and for the strength of the expansive wave of the upheaval which was whipping all its components.**

# The jewels of Saint Lucy

*S*aint Lucy is venerated with great devotion in her church in Bay Boulevard, an area of aristocratic residence, with an aura of the Mafia, and of a civic order appropriate to the kind of an urban section where everybody wants to live in peace and security. The temple is of a Gothic style belonging to the first half of the twentieth Century, built with the alms of the Italian immigrants who wanted to impress the mark of their faith in the middle of the mess of the powerful melting pot in that golden époque. The church shows in its façade a rose window which is considered the most artistic in the Continent because of its audacious circumference, the celestial court printed in its glasses, with such a vivid colors that make many onlookers believe that they are looking at a sacred swarming, and the stony carving is so fine and immaterial, but consistent to the point that it stands the north winds that blow furiously from the open bay.

Though the image of Saint Lucy is not only valued for the devotion of the faithful and for the jewels that it carries, but also for the stained glasses in the lateral walls of her temple, inserted in the monumental ogives. In these stained glasses just Italian Saints are printed, like Saint Rocco, "il Poverello", Saint Catherine of Siena, Saint Patrick. And at the feet of these stained glasses the names of the donating families are written, all unmistakable Italian names, as Gallo, Colombo, Merino, Di Pietro, Bonno, Bardino, and for this reason everybody considers this place a sacred sanctuary of the devoted and altruistic Mafia. This is a temple with power and with power emanation, which imposes to the visitor and to the passerby a reverential awe, since everybody is aware that the Mafia here expiates its misdeeds and tries to bless its plots. At least this is the elf which makes many become suspicious about the cult offered to Saint Lucy here inside.

The jewels of Saint Lucy basically are four: a diamond of the thickness of the head of the largest finger of a human hand, which is hanging from each ear with a golden thread, and two eye orbits which she presents in a small tray, found in the mines of El Nevado, in Colombia, and which are two emeralds shaped like the largest ones found in there. These two last are a donation of the eight more powerful enterprises in Little Italy, in the lower Manhattan, and the two errands were donated by the two families which have hated each other until death, with terrible vendettas among them, the Gallos and the Colombos, in the occasions of the reconciliation through the marriage of a boy from the ones and a girl from the other. But it has to be noted that the diamonds hanging from the ears were a donation from a family friend to the Gallos or to the Colombos. The great love of the Italian colony in New York is the Saint Lucy's jewels in the church of her name, in Brooklyn. This love endures through the generations already merged in the melting pot and there are entire families which organize pilgrimages from very distant places to venerate the Blessed Image of Saint Lucy and contemplate the marvelous effect on her of those unique jewels.

Suddenly, the alarm spread in that Italian colony. Nobody

wanted to believe the news, brought by the *The Daily News*: "The jewels of Saint Lucy have been robed". Its text had the image of the statue of Saint Lucy in the back ground… without its jewels! And everybody who was of Italian ascent or who knew the hidden psychological snag which involved the binomial Saint Lucy-jewels felt that the news was burning the oxygen for breathing. That was an omen of great evils, since that news was announcing that terrible public disasters were approaching, some national disasters and also international ones of an apocalyptic scope.

And everybody was in panic, because the blow to the Mafia was scandalous. And nothing is more lethal than the offended Mafia; yet more than offended, humiliated, put in a public derides. For this reason many who rather could be considered in a neutral corner, were laughing to themselves because the company of the organized crime that had so great fame of invulnerable, certainly now was accusing cracks and it was a dangerous monster with mud feet, like a giant who, with some push, could be demolished. Everybody was expecting that the Mafia would act with promptness to wash its face, not caring at all about the means it would use to do it.

In the parish of Saint Lucy the telephone was ringing all morning long begging for some information about the case. And many of those calls had the evil intention to see how the pastor reacted in front of the poisonous robbery and what was he doing to preserve his canonical balance upon the dividing line between the organized crime and the devotion to the saints. To the extent that Monsignor Bordini, the pastor, forbid all in the house to get the telephone and connected it to the answering machine, where he himself recorded the simple and evasive message: "This is an outer day for the clergy. Please, call tomorrow. Have many blessings from the glorious Saint Lucy".

But it happened that one of the calls belong to the Most Excellent Mugavero in person, Bishop of Brooklyn and Queens, an American of Italian ascent. The official Church names an Anglo Saxon Bishop to the Dioceses of New York, integrated by an extensive Irish colony, and Anglo Saxon, and an Italian one for the Diocese of Brooklyn in consideration to the complex Latin colony. So, Bishop Mugavero was in chock when he did not get any answer from the telephone of the parish. He could not conceive to be treated like one of the many, like a simple faithful, and he imagined ugly omens about the case which was causing so negative impact in the mass media. The official Church reputation was in danger in front on the bunch of millions of local observers and of those around the world. Ready the cut the disturbance in its basis, and to restore his episcopal rights upon institutions and persons, the Bishop ordered his secretary to drive him to Saint Lucy's.

They were there before they even thought, considering the heavy traffic in the rush hour. When the Bishop was walking fast in the side walk of the garden which surrounds the building of the church straight to the rectory, he was so disappointed in seeing the image of Saint Lucy upon an improvised altar, very coarse by the way, without her jewels and, in a little tray where she keeps her two emeralds, which are her eyes, a black pistol like a poisonous fish and of an exaggerated size. And hanging from the altar cloth, there was a poster which read: "The Italian Association demands that the Saint Lucy's jewels come back to her today".

The Bishop thought he could not survive such a sacrilegious gathering. A gentleman muttered within his ear shut: ("My goodness! The Italian Association is the Mafia!"). The Bishop cried: "This pistol has to be removed right now from this tray!"

Two men appeared immediately, dressed with rigorous black three piece-suit, hat and necktie of the same color, with the background of a white shirt. They looked exactly like Al Capone. The Bishop lost his breath; two old Sicilian ladies who were coming to visit Saint Lucy cried out in sympathy with the

Bishop, and they made the sign of the cross speeding upon their bodies. The two men said nothing; they looked at heavens beyond the roofs of the houses and upon the boughs of the oaks, moving the fingers of their hands in sector where the pistol is kept. Like that one who nothing is doing.

"This is exactly the way the Mafia acts!" somebody raised his voice in the opposite sidewalk.

Notice which spread a reverential fear among the curious observers; whoever said it knew what he was saying and was saying it with a devout accent. The Bishop got a support in his words and was able to walk to the rectory, in which door he read the same text of the poster in the outside altar. And read it too in the door of the church. Stopped again by the capital sentence formulated straight out from the sacred place, he moved his sight to the crowd of the faithful who were observing him from the other sidewalk and he felt in the middle of two streams of turbulent waters –everything so different from when he arrived to a town to be a pastor, ready to spread so many blessings. He went ahead oppressed by a feeling of impotence, with that bitterness in the heart caused by the coldness from the part of those who are depending on your care of a good shepherd. He stepped in the rectory and fell on the sofa of the office. He asked for the pastor and the answer came that he went fishing to the Lake Hopatkong, with some friends.

Early, the following morning, he got a message from Mnsgr. Bordini, the pastor of Saint Lucy's, announcing him that last night, before midnight, the stolen jewels were back to the correspondent place of the image of Saint Lucy.

"This is the way the Mafia acts!" he commented, as an official statement from the bishop of the diocese, making an unconscious citation of the words spoken by that gentleman in the sidewalk.

# Lapu-Lapu

*A*fter two years of been ordained to the priesthood, the Rev. Fred Zanca was assigned to the parish of Saint Martin of Tours, in Babylon, Long Island. He was a dreamer, a man with many ideals, friendly to the weak, with a dense beard and lacking care about the shining of his shoes. He was an associate pastor, there, a section where many races were gathered from the planet, among the most different because of the language, the color of the skin and the human quality. There abounded the Asiatic, with the majority of the Indians and Philippines. Fred spoke only English and with just this language he was doing so well to such diverse community. Yet he was wishing more for himself and was doing his best to learn Tagalog at least, the language of the Philippines, who were trusted to his particular attention and they were the most numerous ethnic group in the parish.

The Indians and the Brazilians, had their own native priest to take care of them, and he many times assisted to their celebration and was filled with holly envy seeing how his two mates were talking to their own citizens a language which really got into their hearts. It was then when he was reaffirming his intention to learn Tagalog. He knew he was not that good to learn languages, yet he was ready to go ahead and not allow to be discouraged by any prejudice or by any laziness, be this one personal or somebody else's.

In this way, after two month of being in the head of his faithful, he had saluted them in Christmas Night with their *Maligayan Pasko,* and this was making him happy, because he could see how it was answered with joy by the heterogenic audience that Night was feeling the church. And after a couple of weeks, he had improved a lot, since he knew three or four salutes more, and in every homily to them alone he said expressions in Tagalog which he elaborated previously with a friend. Yes, he was encouraged by the complacency the Philippines were showing with his daring expressions in Tagalog.

Meanwhile a magazine from Maryknoll came to his hands in which an interesting report about the social and missioner activity carried out in the island of Cebu, one of the extensive in the archipelago of the Philippines, where the news appeared that the local authorities had removed the statue of Magallanes from its pedestal, right in the place where he was killed by the native Lapu-Lapu, and had placed the statue of the native instead. For the mentality of Fred Zanca the news was sensational. It impressed him that much, that on reading it he wanted to applaud it by his hands, in spite of being alone in his room. It was an act of amends to the Philippine Citizens, in the long run it was an homage to their identity, making justice to them, honoring whom had to be honored and not an unjust invader, because of his fidelity to the land and the favor made to his fellow citizens. "For heaven sake, bravo!" he cried.

Excited by the philosophy of the news, he thought well about it and elaborated a strategy to inform his folk and surprise them.

Telling them one by one would not be exciting as informing all the community at mass. He was thinking all the week long to insert it in Sunday homily in an easy and convenient way, in which he would use that theme of Asia and of Jesus Christ: "I have come to redeem the captives, to make free the oppressed and to preach the Good News to the poor". The announcement would have to phases: the narration of the fact as an example, like nothing he was saying, yet fast, vivid, and then saying a prayer for the hero, within the prayers of the faithful, while summoning him to liberate the oppressed peoples by the powerful.

And so he did on Sunday. During his homily he surely was in the watch scrutinizing the faces and their reactions when he mentioned the magic of the double Lapu-Lapu. And he could see that the name really caused an impact: many burst into laughing and some in the audience even muttered a couple of words with the next in the seat, man or woman. Yet everybody was looking at him, satisfied and half laughing, and following with avidity whatever he was saying about the change of statues in that pedestal. To the extent that he was so happy and excited that a couple of words were altered in his throat and could not leave outside of it. And even, at the moment of mentioning the Patron of the Church, Saint Martin of Tours, after the Blessed Virgin and her husband, Saint Joseph, he mentioned "Saint" Lapu-Lapu too, with all the intention of canonizing him before hand, yes, because of his fact of heroic sanctity. Being so concentrated in his celebration, Fred was able to detect the whisper of laughing and of short comments in the audience after he declared a Saint the native Lapu-Lapu.

He never dismissed the faithful with a spirit so extol and with so much empathy to their identity like that time; another grateful whispering from those who were waving their hands to him, with an ample smile, with oriental discretion. He walked to the sacristy like not stepping in the solid ground, grateful to the magazine Maryknoll because it provided to him an occasion to be father and pastor of those sheep so far away from their homes and in a way which really reached to their hearts.

The following Saturday Fred blessed the marriage of a Philippine couple, in the parish. The memory was still persisting in him and had his soul scented with the happy odor of the last Sunday celebration. He abstained, in the presence of so numerous diverse attendants, from mentioning again the hero, because many could not be Philippine, but he was feeling in his element; he was considering that the influx of that so historic name had made him very fraternal with that race, and given him the charisma to understand them and of vibrating in unison with them. After the liturgical celebration of the wedding, all went to have lunch to a Philippine restaurant.

And there happened that one of the most solid dishes of that banquet, and at the same time boastful, it has to be said, was a roasted fish long more than a foot, which came to the table with a strange tic of life inserted in its head, with a mouth of a lophius, with its open, irritated and salacious eyes, in a platter and surrounded by a not identified side-dish. Yet it had a soft and exquisite pulp, in spite of his ugly aspect in its appearance on the table. As Fred could see enough, it was of the high preference of the natives. A platter on each table and all cleared it up, may be everybody feeling his portion too short.

"What a delicious fish!" Fred commented in one of the presiding tables.

"It is our national fish, gotten from the see which surrenders the archipelago" a young Philippine lady explained, with an effable approach, without any small piece of pride.

"And being ugly as it is!" Fred commented, hiding the intention of flattering the girl.

"It is the providence of our poor families" declared her husband, speaking and showing the piece of fish which he had in his mouth, chewing it. "As a matter of fact, the mass of the

Philippines survives, in more than a fifty per cent, due to this fish".

"And how do you call it?" Fred asked, always with that little bit of intention to flatter them.

"Lapu-Lapu" the answer came, easy and without any hesitation.

# The compass of
# the Hazidim

Cecilio Arroyo was a photographer who had the charisma to get the tic of the human beings that reveals the most recondite felling of a soul. In this aspect his photos were a mirror of the moral quality of the subject on each one, they were a reflex of the little miseries or of the good virtues of his soul. It was a professional obsession going behind his object, a man or a woman, looking for the revealing moment, fragile and precarious like a wing of a butterfly, absorbed as the naturalist does looking for the most rare and unclassified bug. Through his life he had caused more than one mocking smile, in the open street, for his fastness to bring his hands in front of his face, to shoot a strange contraction, a cry, a hiccup by a passarby.

He was working as a photographer through a decade in San Juan, Puerto Rico, and in rural areas, and though he insisted on bettering his capacities and his product, the retribution was miserable, he was not improving his budget. He came to the

United States poor as a beggar, yet rich in ideals and ready to
become a famous professional of the camera. Because he had made
more than one exposition there, in his native town, and many
had commented him that his photos showed a strong personal
print, it is to say, that day included the elf of a diabolic sense of the
man and of human life, which had to be read with good doses of
psychiatry. He came to Brooklyn to the flat of his aunt, the sister
of his mother, Doña Milagros, who was renting it in Borough Park
and was living there depending on the Welfare, by herself and
having four children in Puerto Rico, who constantly were open
their mouths to her as a nest of little birds.

The name of the place sounded interesting to him, for being
cryptic and unknown. The name was making him understand
from the beginning, that he had to fight against the new and
exotic ambient, may be even hostile, and sure unpredictable. And
this was challenging him. It was a cosmopolitan district, like in
all of New York, and of course he would meet all kinds of persons,
there, of any kind of character and moral, and they would make
an excellent field of different faces for his camera, unique, unseen
before; people willing to tend a hand to him, and other people
trying to hurt him; and even careful with those willing to help
him, because it will always be exploring his soul for their own
interest.

He arrived to his aunt place at night, tire and battled by the jet
lag. But the following morning he wanted to get out to the street
and make the first exploration, with the camera hanging from
his neck. He was pretty sure that he would meet some Spanish
guy, to say hello and chat with him to get the first orientations or
some photograph store where some Spanish was, acquainted in
photography and get professional advice about the matter.

He was surprised by the silence in the street in that first hour.
There was not any birds cheeping, gathered in the corpulent trees
of the tropics, or sultriness in the ambient. He remembered the

hour of the frenetic *chachalacas* from the trees; their morning delirium there was causing him an uncomfortable emotional emptiness in his soul. The silence was a vehicle for the roaring of the cars and some blowing of the horns heard now and then. His attention was pulled by the silent movement of a series of black guys walking in the sidewalks and disappearing in the corners; they were men dressed with a rigorous black overcoat, wearing a rigorous black hat with ample wings and black shoes not making any noise on the pavement. But, wearing a coat...? It was just in the beginning of the month of September.

That novelty was so pleasant to him. He forgot the camera, hanging from his shoulder. Those concentrated, mute men bewildered him. Black from top to bottom, obviously not because of some decease, but for religious reasons, and those many in every direction like a bunch of ants, with another quantity of women dressed like them in rigorous black color, rather young, silent like them and going straight to their goal, differed a lot from the other people moving in the street, Spanish, American, Black, Oriental.

He remembered the camera when, in a corner, met an individual with that dress, a fat man, almost obese, walking rather fast, with two corkscrews curls in each temple, moving at the wind produced by his march. Cecilio mad the spontaneous gesture of bringing the apparel before his eyes to shoot it to him –those corkscrews curls alone merited photo!– but the man made to him an ugly face of refusal, of repulsion, and hid his face from the camera, while making the impulse to attack him, if he persisted on it. Cecilio became petrified, looking at that aggressive reaction. The passerby would never salute him or looked at him, according to his attitude continuing aggressive in all the manner of getting away... Something so normal in his Country, to say hello to the citizens, though unknown, to take a photo! Cecilio could observe that the guy had to clods of coffee in his hairy mustache and to more in his beard. And still looking at him getting away, the man turned to the right in a corner beyond the one in which he was standing and he lost track of him.

Later on he commented the case with his aunt.

"Be careful with these people, because they do not love anybody and whatever you do to them will be interpreted as an act of conspiracy against their security" the lady summoned him.

Cecilio was so astonished. All in all was an ugly omen for his future life in that so inhuman ambient. He did not understand it.

"But the fact is that he carried two corkscrews of a young lady in each side of his face..." he insisted, disconcerted. "What those corkscrews curls meant in the face of a man"?

"What they mean is not your business, believe me. All of them wear it. You follow your way and here do not wonder about anything, and do not care what people are doing, if not It will be evil to you" the lady was very serious.

"But you do not say to me what they mean..."

"I say again +to you that they could mean whatever they mean. After some time of being here, you'll considerer silly to want to know what the other people do and think, you'll see it!" she was persisting on him, willing to be eyed.

"And what's the name of these people?"

"They are called the Hasidim... They believe a lot in God, they follow their way and do not bother anybody and don't want to be bothered" she was trying to satisfy him.

But he was far away to be convinced. He was lost about the whole issue. Though he did not like to insist upon the aunt and put obstacles to her kindness trying to clarify things which overcame him. He made her believe that he was satisfied and got ready to explore by himself that interesting and different world from what he had witnessed so far in his life, to explore it and make a culture to enrich himself.

The following day he got to the street ready to wide his knowledge of the environment. And he saw the same situation than the day before: many individuals dressed in rigorous black overcoats up and down the street –some of them circulated beside him and they wore the same corkscrew curls that they were wearing yesterday– rushing, silent, introverted women, some elegant dresses, yet not flamboyant, some Spanish people... He was crossing the street and felt a shadow upon him that forced him to close his eyes and stop in order not to crash with... the same fat guy of yesterday! He even felt the scent of kitchen from that black coat, something that was blocking his nose! He was looking at him while walking ahead in the sidewalk. The subject had ignored him totally, coldly. Cecilio got the impression, from the attitude of the man, that the universe belonged to him; they had been in the verge of crashing and the silent guy said nothing excusing himself, he did not even looked at him and, if Cecilio does not stop the other would drag him away like a machine without any feeling for the living persons. The foreigner did not deserve any attention, he did not deserve a simple salute, not even a smile to the apology he, Cecilio, said to him.

Cecilio did not comment anything to his aunt. He kept it in his mind, he was ruminating it by himself; the lived scene, the coldness of that guy for the strangers, his unusual behavior, his external religious paraphernalia were segregating to him intrigue and unrest. He did not agree to it; he was not a practical believer, but he demanded the human ethics of the respect to the others and the consideration to the brother, no matter how he is poor and unknown, what he considered fundamental in any faith, as he heard it commented in his visits to the church in San Juan.

From that moment he decided to find out the meaning of the things those people were practicing. He did not doubt that his personage was the epitome of the race, its key example; he would shoot his camera to the man several times, without being seen by him, some "technical" shuts, very expressive, and with them he would start his professional job. He would make a report about *The Hasidim in Borough Park* and he would send it to the main Spanish newspaper in New York and to some love magazine that are been sent from Miami to Latin America and in this way he could become known as a perverse photographer and a penetrating newsman.

The following day, more or less at the same time he had met yesterday his hero, he was watching beneath the threshold of the building where his aunt lived and, as soon as he saw the black bunch crossing the street and turning around the next corner, he walk behind him, ready to follow him wherever he would go. He rushed to approach him and kept walking several meters behind him, paying much attention to his itinerary.

The man got into a subway station and he did the same, after speeding more to be able to get into the same train he would take, in the next wagon. And it was hard to him, to Cecilio, because the rush and the crashes among the passengers to get into the train kept it waiting enough for him to step in. It was the early morning rush hour and it was a mess. Any way he could control his man through the glass door between the two wagons, his black hat of ample wings, among the many heads, hats and arms holding the hoods over the seated passengers to keep the balance, and sometimes he could see a portion of his hairy red face in contrast with the rigorous black of the hat and the coat.

When he saw him walking his way through the open door, in a stop, he did the same and followed him among the many bodies in the platform, always at a prudent distance. Suddenly he realized that upon him the fearful structures were getting into heavens and he could not resist the impulse to look at them and to grasp for a moment the prodigious effect that caused those urban monsters; when turned his eyes to his man, he just could see the hairy black hat crossing the street in middle of a crowd of heads, and he blamed himself because he was risking losing his track and spoiling his good occasion. He was not sure that the man was his hero and not another like him. He ran to cross the street, as the other did, and had to do it hearing severe corn blows by angry drivers because he was crossing in the red light of the corner lights.

He could see that upon his head the flag of his Country, but he could not pay any attention to it; he was in the Avenue of the Americas. The man was turning to the right in the corner and he had to run again to be able to see that he, in the middle of two more Hazidim, was opening the door of a store and was stepping in and letting the door close in the face of the others, not caring at all about them.

It was a commerce that had an extraverted display case, with much precious glass and many jewels in its many shelves. He opened his eyes like oranges at the sight of so many diamonds upon a layer of dark blue velvet. That was a strike of opulence really smashing the taste. His eyes were pulled to contemplate the iridescence of some pieces like *chachalaca's* eggs, but he could not forget what was going on inside with his hero, doubting about staying there and looking through the glass or stepping in, as a client. He looked deep inside and the man had vanished somewhere. Damn you! He could notice inside a silent rush, a hidden ambition of clients analyzing jewels and of clerks praising them, like they were perspiring, with a latent nerve. People were stepping in, in that store, and getting out, constantly. Finally he stepped in, like one of so many.

He was chocked as seeing two policemen standing on each side of the entrance door, checking strictly all the movements of the clients. But on seeing him, they placed all the attention in his person, but not turning completely their faces to him. He read mistrust in those eyes, he detected on them the old racial prejudice toward himself, because of his aspect of Spanish and of a poor guy. But he immediately discovered his hero seated in a chair, back to him, in one of several compartments beyond the main desk and in front of the shelves containing so many diamonds. He withdrew immediately the camera from his shoulder ready to shoot a photo to him... yet not seeing through it the black shadow of the man, but the shadow of a hand that obstructed the objective. It was the hand of one of the two guardians. The same man grasped his arm and accompanied him to the outside door.

"No pictures allowed in here! So, get lost!" the official said to him, while saying good bye, but not in a polite manner.

He thought that the pictures within there could rather be welcome for propaganda reasons... He did not understand, he was considering everything of bad taste. Well, it was because they saw that he was a poor man, incapable to buy anything of those marvels! He stood in the middle of the sidewalk, alienated, not knowing what to do next. For sure that man in there was fulfilling a job of high technology, like cutting diamonds, value them, to fix them in supports of refined goldsmith. A picture of that guy, intended in his labor, would be of a sensational interest, in contrast to his dress of a religious fanatic, who seemed rather a penitent, and for many even of a beggar.

Then he decided to orient himself in order to return there after having elaborated some strategy. He looked upon the store and saw a large poster with large bronze letters that read: *World Diamond Center.* He experienced a kind of reverential fear and got off the strong irradiation of that store. In the corner he could see that it was the Forty Seven Street, between Fifth and the Americas Avenues. But he resented so much to go back home with his empty camera; after his daring trip, he found it unjust. Battled by this feeling he went back to the store, and after a look inside through the show window, trying carefully no to be seen by the policemen, he saw his man in that compartment, though just getting his profile, but he considered that enough to get the two curls of one temple, the glasses, a black skullcap that now was covering his head instead of the black hairy hat and a good section of his pharaonic nose. And flash! Flash two times. And right away took off fast in the sidewalk toward the subway station, not turning around to see a policeman chasing him. Before getting into the station he turned around again and he saw nobody being alert or chasing him. And this comforted him.

But his surprise was bitter when that evening he developed the spool of photos and realized that the counter, the clients, the lights, that compartment... were very visible, but not at all his man! The absolute absence of his main objective! He did not understand it; everything seemed to be a play of witches. Except that the man would bend down to get something fallen in the ground at that very moment...

Nevertheless he was not a guy made for discouragement. Now he would try to find the place where the hero was living and surely he would find the way to get some pictures of him, which would show him immerse in his domestic environment. It had to become a gorgeous report!

Renewed in spirit, that same evening at the calculated time the Hasidim could come back home from his work, Cecilio was walking up and down around that corner where the guy was turning to go to the subway station and, when he saw him walking among the many, walked from behind to make up with him just in order to learn where he finally entered, but not carrying the camera, wearing other pants and another shirt. He followed him six or seven blocks, always walking in Seventh Avenue, and finally could see the man getting into a single house surrounded by a small garden, not much well kept, with a garage in the ground floor, a flat, a terrace upon the garage with an iron handrail and two windows upon the flat, that well could be another flat or a simple attic upon the main flat.

But what was all he was seeing in the neighboring houses? The terraces and even the balconies contained a kind of high boxes of not an identified material, three or four times larger than the wrapper of a refrigerator. And in every box some people were seated, or standing, having a cup of coffee or of tee, in their hands, or simply chatting, as it was a children's hut done by them like a toy, a lady who made crochet, a family head reading a book nodding frequently, children making their homework, a family mother setting the table, a young lady playing her violin. Everything was done in silence and in a strange festive desolation in the street.

He would ask some passer-by the meaning of that phenomenon. His aunt explained it to him later on: "It's because of the feast the Lewes name *Sukkot,* which remembers the fact that those who were walking in the desert, in their march from Egypt to the Promised Land, had to live in tends, according to the Old Testament. It was a fantastic idea and he would write a great narration of every detail of that feast and exhibit gorgeous photos, which would express the contrast between the opulence in diamonds and the puerile idea, almost ridiculous, of that feast. The last he could witness was his hero getting into the box in his terrace making a lot of head bends reading some book which, according to the aunt, had to be the Bible.

The following day, at evening, Cecilio was again in the section of Borough Park. Excited, concentrated in his theme, pulled by the uniqueness of that celebration. As practicing it, and still far away from the place where his hero lived in order not to be noticed by him, he shut several times the camera to objectives in balconies and terraces where Hasidim in action were.

Then he walk until de sidewalk near the house of his man, and he was so surprised on seeing him within the box in the terrace and speeding making head bends, according to what all the men around were making. He reached into the next corner and turned around as it was the most normal thing in the world. He prepared the camera according to the least requisites for its good functioning. And went back by the same sidewalk, looking indifferent, with the camera hanging in his chest ready to shoot it two, three, four times, according to his experience in the degree of focusing and of looking for the best angle, suppressing the gesticulation not to alarm anybody. In the long run, that evening he finished the whole spool of thirty-five exposures, to make sure.

He was having dinner with his aunt, happy, commenting the fact to her, and suddenly the doorbell rang, short, demanding. He went to open it and found two tall policemen, wearing a blue uniform and both having a large pistol in their cincture.

"Are you the one who is chasing Mr. Jacob Prebat to photograph him?" asked one of them, a Puerto Rican, after saluting him politely.

Cecilio was petrified.

"Yes" he could finally answer, with panic.

"Then this is a legal worn in order that you stop chasing the gentleman. If you continue doing it, the case will go to the court. Understood? Good night!"

The two officials took off, affable, and relaxed having fulfilled their duty.

He looked at them, like a mommy, while they were vanishing in the elevator.

"What is it?" his aunt asked him, alarmed.

"I was doing it to start working and to make a living…" he excused himself afterwards.

"Don't do it! Be very careful, because these people are very powerful and they can bring you to prison!" the aunt was warning him, terrified.

At night Cecilio developed the spool. Very hesitant about what he was doing. He could realized that in all the photos people were missing, except a rascal who was getting away, in a photo, and a fat lady who was bending to the ground, in another.

And in all of those shut to the beloved hero, he was absent, not a small portion of his fat body appeared on them.

The mystery upon the case bewildered a long time the soul of
Cecilio. Until a Puerto Rican friend to whom he was commenting
the fact, informed him that the Hasidim believe that "photos suck
their souls out from their bodies". They believe that photography
takes a part of their personality out of them".

# Spirit of solidarity

he area of Cypress Hills is an aristocratic one. Hardly blunts in it one of those skyscrapers or any of those lower buildings that are made off baked clay, without any ornamental motif that prevents them to look like human cages and are called *projects*. The professionals of more prestige establish in this borough, those who in the old continent would be called *liberal arts*, as to say doctors in medicine, lawyers, newsmen, doctors in science, diplomats. The neighborhood is clean, it is safe, the streets are clean too, the houses are generally for a single family, they have porticoes in the front, they are surrounded by trees and gardens treated by professional gardeners, with loans of grass which inhale a fresh breath. Surely this is the section more idyllic all over the town. It is the more human, too.

This was the section selected by Mr. Kevin Harrison to settle in with his family when he came to this country. He was called by Saint John's University, from Tanzania, because he was an expert in young African literatures. He was a descendant from a North American slave who escaped to Tanzania in search of his human roots. Saint John's needed him to teach three consecutive courses of the African literature to the young students and of the universal literature of the letters faculty and of modern languages. The young man became a PHD in the University of Oxford, where he revealed himself as a literary talent and having a vast knowledge of the Pan Africanism in its historic and intellectual aspects. Mr. Kevin pointed out to all who talked with him about his immigrant condition that he abandoned his natal Country just for those three years, to get acquainted with the national American spirit and its culture in order that then he could be helpful to its land and to the their fellow citizens.

Kevin had a nice character, open, sensitive to the person, in his Country he cooperated in several philanthropic activities, such as Doctors without Frontiers, Universal Clowns, conceived to help his fellow citizens to get rid of the primitivism. By means of this habit, Kevin had developed a character full of faith in the goodness of the human family and in the peaceful accord between the different races, cultures, languages, credos and national interests of the diverse antipodes who integrate it. Kevin was a solidary spirit, builder of peace, incapable to hurt the less dignified creature. And what he professed, expected without any effort and with politeness from the rest of the world.

Once he had settle in Queens, his first diligence was to matriculate his children in the school that offered more guaranties of discipline and effectiveness in the formation of the infants, in order that his own could assimilate, from childhood the same ideals of their father. He found it no far away from his new home in the institution named John Fitzgerald Kennedy, which gathered the cream of the children of that neighborhood. The first day of class he and his wife accompanied the children to the reception office and were impressed by the easiness air, of the joy and of climate of welcome reigning in there. Once the children left under the authority of the teachers, he took off to Saint John's

University, where the preparations for the beginning of the course were already on, while the wife returned home to take care of the domestic tasks. Husband and wife said goodbye with a look of love and of mutual intelligence because the children were left in good hands and in an excellent shelter.

Two days had elapsed and, arriving home in the evening, Kevin realized that his oldest boy, Marvin, ten years old, had an eye hurt, all blue color, within a brown circle of bloody lymph. The child looked defeated, downcast. The wife, standing back to him in the sinker, at the bottom and in the middle of two columns that separated the kitchen from the dining room, turned around to welcome him making a visible effort no to allow the full cry burst out of her mouth.

"Son, what is it?" he asked the child.

"Father, a white boy punched me in the eye because I was defending Rosemary and Jeannette when he was ready to harass them" the boy answered him, trying not to cry.

The two little sisters looked at the father asking protection and burst into crying. Kevin looked with much attention the eye of his son; the brown and the blue colors made an ugly combination, like of meat dried in the sun, the pupil was black, the eyelids had attached small pieces of solid fluid and all he eye appeared swollen.

"Did you counter attack him?" he wanted to know, very strict.

"No, father, I didn't, because I did not want to make it bigger, in spite he was persisting in saying that "they did not want dogs or blacks in the school!" And I had to restrain me because many other children, boys and girls, were backing him".

The following day father, mother and children went back to the school. It was the time children enter the school; the habitual joy was reigning there, between the ups and downs of the parents and the teachers going to their places. Kevin took all the family to the reception office. He said hello to two lady teachers seated in the respective desk, who were paying much attention to what was going on in the corridors with so many children walking in them. Kevin showed the face of his child to them.

"See what happened yesterday. Here, in the school" told them.

They both looked at the child and made no comment. They lowered their eyes to the papers in the desk, surely embarrassed and not willing to judge the case.

"I demand an explanation from you!" Kevin said to them, with perfect control, yet with energy.

"If you have some complaint, go to see the director of the school" said to him one of the two ladies.

Kevin saw the poster hanging from the top of the door of the director's office and stepped in with all his family.

"I want to see the Director of the school" he begged a lady teacher who at that moment was opening the door of the office.

"He is not in and he'll not be in through the rest of the day" the lady answered him, fast, rapid, a little bit angry.

To the extent that Kevin suspected that all was a lie. The lady vanished inside, leaving him in his cruel doubt. His son claimed his attention.

"Daddy, this is the one who punched me in my eye!" he pointed the boy out to him who was walking in the corridor with another two.

Kevin looked at him very severely. He stood in his way.

"You insulted my daughters and hurt my son!" confronted the boy.

This looked at him for a moment, surprised. He was a little bit taller that the average of the pupils, but spongy and heavy. Immediately he made with his lips a face of repulse to the man who was questioning him and looked at him and at all with arrogance.

"Get out of here!" shouted to them all, moving back two steps to include all the family in his challenge and his scorn. "We don't want here dogs or negroes!"

Kevin raised his arm to punish him with a slap, but controlled himself. At the same time the voice of a lady teacher resounded in order he stopped it.

"Don't do it!"

The rascal had made a fist and was looking at him with sarcasm in the middle of the other two, as a bully secure about his power.

"Touch me if you want that we kill you all!" he challenged him meaning all his family. "I know here in my house my daddy keeps his pistol, to eliminate the blacks who bring their asses to the schools which are just for white citizens! And my friends have their pistols, too!"

Kevin could not believe what he was hearing. He conceived panic to the little despots. And he conceived respect to the bunch of rascals who were coming to see what was going on there, silent and with hostile faces. Then he looked around to ask protection and explanations from a teacher, form a guard –and he saw none. Then he stretched his arms upon his children and walk with them and his wife out of the school.

He did not send them again to the school. He was thinking about what could be the best to do. He thought to send them to a religious school, more expensive, private, where he could get respect to the color of his skin.

Meanwhile he was not losing his time and he was writing an article of complaint, with the grievance his disappointment was oozing, where he was denouncing the brutal abuse his children had suffered and sent it to a local newspaper, *The Daily Mirror*, to which he was subscribed and seemed to him rather balanced and wise.

His writing was published three days later in that newspaper, while he was all busy looking for a new school and to open the course in the University. He had been a whole day out of the house and at evening he was seated on a recliner in the leaving room, reading his article and congratulating himself for having said things straight and clear, revealing to the neighbors how much he was hurt by the discrimination suffered by his children. Fully absorbed by his ideas, weighing them, he saw down in the bottom of the lowered shadow of the window, how some light was dancing proceeding from some fire in the square.

Highly bewildered, he went to the window and raised its shadow. In the center of the square a cross was burning. Around the cross there were several human figures, dressed in white tunics and their head covered with a long hood, white too. All of them with their eyes fixed on him, framed by the open window; all the eyes were sparkling with the fire. In a distance of twelve or thirteen feet there were standing three men dressed in white tunic and covered with the white hood also, but with the face section opened and showing their beards like the one of Jesus Crist, but denying with their furious eyes full of hatred his Gospel and any principle of humanity. Kevin not even could lower the shadow; the sudden, dantesque vision was petrifying him there and he was looking like a painted man by force in a wall.

"Get out of our place the ones who disturb peace among us!" shouted to him the man who was in the middle of the three, with a tune of hatred.

Kevin could not answer back or even breathe, like in a nightmare. Those words were hurting deeply his heart. That theme in the mouth of citizens who presented a good aspect was upsetting and humiliating him. The panic was keeping him speechless.

"The Ku-Klux-Klan!" his wife moaned besides him, while he was lowering the shadow of the window, to prevent her from seeing that vision.

Then she had to support him and seat him in the recliner.

"We cannot be here anymore, my dear" she murmured him, caressing his wet and perspiring forehead with her hand, crying like a child. The lives of our children and our own are in stake".

The following day, in the early norming, all the family was in the airport Kennedy, ready to fly back to Tanzania.

# The Penitent

That Sunday had been intense in liturgical celebrations and Santos Romero was feeling tired in the evening. He celebrated alone all the services of the afternoon, with the youngsters and the children, plus the rather bourgeois and cold evening mass, assisted by those speaking English who were resting on Sunday or who made the effort of leaving home or breaking some entertainment. He had put the collection into the safe of the office of the rectory and now he was enjoying a coke, seated in a recliner in front of the television set watching the football game between the Chicago Bulls and the Forty Niners of San Francisco. It was an excellent entertainment for his taste of a young man. He was dressed in shorts and underwear because of the warm weather; he was tall, corpulent and was perspiring as one of the players in the screen. While absorbing the ups and downs of the play, he felt asleep. He was on duty, he was by himself, the other priests and the service personnel were off enjoying the ambiguous weather of Sunday evening.

Suddenly the doorbell rang twice. There was no office service, no parish services unless it was an emergency. Anyway Santos loved to contact people and he did not like do as the others who, in these occasions, just opened the small window in the door to see who it was, to see whether they open the door or not. It was a very dressed young man, with not a definite expression, may be a little bit worried, asking him to hear his confession.

"These ordinary services are offered on Saturday afternoon during an hour" he informed the boy.

"Please, I am a great sinner" the other objected. "I carry a bunch of ugly sins and it would be impossible to sleep this night to me if I did not get rid of them all. Please".

Santos invited him to enter a small room, used *ad hoc,* and signaled him to seat in a chair, or to kneel down, whatever he preferred. The boy decided for the second offer and kneeled down in the floor, where he adopted an attitude of sincere repentance. Santos was seated beside him in another chair.

The confession of that boy was not "normal", it was vague and divagating. It could be that old paternal systems of education based on bigotry and false Christianity were perverting that soul, victim of undetermined scruples… Santos was listening to him, badly impressed, to be able afterwards to give advice to that pusillanimous conscience and straighten out that tormented soul by the absurd.

"You need a longer therapy than a simple confession" he finally told him. "Now it is too late and we are tired; tomorrow come back at the office hours and we will debate your spiritual recovery, please".

"You are right. It is exactly as you say, father" the boy admitted.

"Now say the act of contrition".

The boy, did not apply the gesture of *mea culpa* to his own chest, but pressed a pistol against father's chest.

"Father let's go to the safe and, if you don't want to die, deliver me the bag that contains all the collections of today" he told him, now very clear and demanding.

The young priest was so surprised by the fact. He looked at the boy while he had the gesture of the absolution in the air, just to see whether he was completing it or not. He did not finish it. Because he saw the guy was extremely serious, rather appearing livid and having a light of hatred in his eye. Santos stood up and the other did the same, while was stepping back in order to control his movements, always keeping the pistol pointed out to his chest.

"I'd never said it!" the reverend confessed him while walking in front of the boy toward the safe, referring to the tenor of the confession.

"I was an altar boy in a church in Pennsylvania and I was never compensated but by a penny", the young man was declaring. "I know quite well what is going on in the rectories … you gather big money. I got up many mornings enduring a bitter cold… Now I am in a big trouble and I need money to overcome it".

"It is not good for you to act in this way. There are many alternatives ways" the priest suggested him, half turning to him.

The boy grunted because he turned around and ordered him to go ahead and don't do it.

"I did not come to listen to your sermons, father".

In front of the safe in the office, Santos lowered his head to remember well the key number of the safe, with his hand applied to the revolving device.

"Reverend, I assure you that I am very serious and mean it!" the boy threatened him, pressing the pistol to his ribs and strictly at the level of the heart". Open it and forget about your comedy!"

The reverend felt naked and moved with panic at the idea of his death. He rotated the device, opened the door of thick iron and five baskets full with dollars appeared to their eyes, correspondent to the five masses of the day.

"Put them all into this sac!" the boy ordered him, referring to the bag that was in a lower shelf to bring the money to the bank once it was counted by the clerks.

The revered bent down with intention of grasping the sac and with the same action he grasped the hand that held the pistol. A shut resounded, instantly. The reverend was no hurt and realized he had all his power concentrated around that death instrument.

The intruder cursed him. He brought his other hand to control the vigor leaving from that corpulent body and from iron hands. The fight was short. And it was vital. Another shut resounded and a silence followed, a crude, suffocated silence; the visitor's body slide down through the solid structure of that of Santos. Who contemplated at his feet the death face of the unknown guy, breathing his last time and he experimented a panic never else felt in his life. He thought he was fainting upon that body in the ground. He imagined for an instant that theory of "mouth to mouth resuscitation", learned in the courses of health and of assistance to the victims of accidents, and kneeled down to practice it to the boy, but the reality taught him it was no avail.

"My God!"

Seeing that thread of blood bleeding from that chest, he begged the Lord to be faithful testimony of the fact. "An ambulance" he shouted as it was asked from somebody around.

He was very upset and ran to the telephone of the office and dialed 411, the police telephone for emergencies, with a syncopated and confused explanation.

Anyway, two officials came in a short period to the rectory. Who rang the street bell and were open almost immediately. They saw him incredulous about his hard situation and not having words for the moment even to welcome them.

The officers looked, first at the body lying in the ground and then looked at him with their eyes and their mouths open, inquiring what all was about. They looked at the open safe, too, and seemed to understand.

"I killed my brother, the child of God!" Santos exclaimed, outraged by a defeat, by a turbulent and anguished mystic. "The Lord will punish me for not been more careful to preserve his life.

"In that very moment just the Lord could tell this a part, not you!" one of the officials comforted him, with professional slyness.

The following morning Santos was still suffering, after a night of cruel insomnia. The dead boy was causing him unutterable pain. And more of it because the parents of the dead could not be found anywhere, or in any list of citizens, and could not be informed about the incidental death, in order that they could cry it with the rest of sensitive persons. The following Monday he asked the pastor to let him celebrate the funeral in the church, to asked pardon from the deceased in any prayer and in every sign to see whether giving the best of himself in his psychosis of guilt and shame for his inability in yesterday's case, in each prayer and in each sign he asked pardon from the cadaver and could find peace and relieve about the accusation which was oppressing him.

The attendance to the funeral was more numerous than habitual. And it was much more variegated. There were many youngsters unusual in the temple, in spite of the hour to be in the institute or in the university. Santos was not looking at anybody from the altar, he was oppressed by the sentiment of guilt and the fact that he could not reconcile to himself, made him believe he could not reconcile with the others. He head a headache, surely he had high fever; he was feeling in his face that the generation in front of him was scrutinizing him with no moderation and was pointing at him as a criminal. He was not looking at them, but he was seeing them moving around the church, groups of punkies, of skinned heads, arrogant like those of Sodom and Gomorra, with rictus of hatred in their hermaphrodite faces. His misfortune was known by all the neighborhood –and surely by all the town– and it was in the hands of the guys with a more racial and tendentious aggressiveness.

At the time of sharing the sign of peace with the audience, as he was used to do in his masses, he got down there and did not go to meet the faithful, but pushed by an abscess of desperation he bent upon the coffin and embraced it, pouring upon words of peace, of sorry, asking pardon and pouring tears.

In that moment somebody raised his voice to him, with insolence. While embracing the coffin, he turned his face around and through the tears he saw the tall figure of a young man who was blaming him in a loud and coarse voice. He was dressed with a black jacket, a pants girdling his legs from top to bottom, wearing high heels shoes.

"Your farce, reverend, deceits nobody!" the unknown was telling him. "Your pantomimes do not clean the blood in your hands of this innocent, who did not consent to your sexual attack!"

With internal rebellion against these words, Santos erected his body and confronted the subject. But he could not find a sacramental word, a straight one to rebuke him. The other was fulminating him with his open eyes in a blue-gray circle of coagulated cosmetic which accentuated his aggressive aspect, within a bunch of curls that was getting thinner if the back, where it was tied with a red ribbon. There was a moment of visual tension between the two of them.

"The fitting-up of the pistol in his hand and the open safe when the police arrives in the office it's a sign of your criminal intention" the unknown was pouring upon him, inexorable in front of the audience, not caring about the celebration. "His blood will be vindicated! All of us will do away with you!"

He was saying it with such a conviction that Santos was smashed. The sensation of being undressed in front of the audience was crushing him, which was breathing hatred, he was feeling it in his skin.

It was impossible to give the sign of peace to anybody else. His spirit, his emotion could not stay in that ambient. He returned to the altar and finished the celebration *per breviorem,* like a cat walking upon live coal. When he imparted the final blessing he had to look at the audience and could realize that he was imparting it upon faces soaked of sarcasm, obscured by the thirst for vengeance; in fact he was blessing the general conviction that he was acting as a pontiff in human sacrifices.

While he was walking to the sacristy, down there a rumor started which grew in a fast *crescendo* and burst into a bunch of bad words –cut by the entrance in the temple of a couple of policemen whom somebody of good will had called. Santos undressed as he could of his garments, abandoned them upon the dressing desk and departed for the dining room of the rectory where his American colleagues, seven or eight, were seated sipping their cups of coffee. He was looking for a support in the vertiginous suspension upon the abyss.

The mates were chatting placidly and eating their fried eggs and bacon. All of them looked at him smiling ironically, friendly or compassionately. Santos found, upon his dish and accessories a local newspaper with large headlines which read: "A catholic priest kills his male lover". The mates were observing his reaction… and he considered that he could expect little support from them

And understood it would be quite difficult for him to prove his innocence. Since he came from a country in South America, he was born in a poor town of a poor and undeveloped country. And his accent in English was poor, too.

# The faint of the watches

he elderly Isaac Goldsmith soled antiques and imported amphoras and pitchers in his store in the Avenue of the Americas. It was a long time that the little store was in that privileged section of Manhattan, in spite of been a small structure without any artistic designed, it's to say, it just had a ground floor room with a simple door to get in and a monstrance window in the side. Isaac's grandfather had installed there in the mere dawn of the commercial expansion of the island of Manhattan and since then on the hairs of the family name had done their best to credit the importance of the firm Goldsmith Imports, Co. The placed was visited by the cream of the aristocracy from New York and by selected tourists. All of them had preferences for the antiques of the ancient Greco-Roman world, of the whole Mediterranean area and for the findings in sank vessels long time ago.

Isaac had been the object of several millionaire invitations to sell his place and he always opposed to it, for lineage reasons, of course, but also because he was old and did not want to see his place demolished by the beast of a large enterprise. And as he was thinking the other stores round were thinking, low and small stores, without ornaments, old, anodyne, yet dynamic, well assorted with exotic, different and precious items. All made a long low line along the block. Besides, the privilege of the place was being so close to Radio City, the Music Hall more important in the world, and in a short distance from the building of the *Life* magazine and from the hotel Hilton. While in the other avenues and streets the buildings were recently new glass and cubism style according to the last tastes of the most audacious urbanism. (The old owners of those low stores were indifferent to the millions of dollars, because they knew they would not enjoy them; they were keeping it inside of the skin, but they did not want to realize it, nor the others realize it).

One day of commercial routine, in the morning, in a clear air after a night of heavy rain, and encouraged by the intense presence in the street of a cosmopolitan crowd excited by the urban scenography, Isaac Goldsmith was surprised, behind his desk, looking at the man who was beating the glass of his shop window with his distinguished walking stick, was opening a whole on it and was stepping inside, to seat on an amphora lower than the rest, belonging to the Minoan civilization. Isaac could not believe what he was looking at. After a short lapse of inaction, he slid to the top of the desk where he had the telephone, got the receiver to dial 411, the one of the police, and put it again in its place, before dialing. My goodness! That man was Salvador Dalí! He knew him personally, he was partner with his brother Ruben Goldsmith of the Art Gallery, The Nouveau Style, in Fifty Seven Street, and the famous eccentric painter had been there many times. In front of the show window there were a bunch of curious citizens looking with fervent passion to the crazy image of Dalí, and growing so fast in number.

Then Isaac agreed to what was going on in his domains. He

was acting with the cleverness of an old cat. The fact could raise the name of his store to a level of fantasy, causing an impact of planetary scope. He was writing in a paper, behind the desk, as nothing was happening around, as nothing was going on in the routine of his busyness. He was looking at the street to see how the bunch of curious citizens was enlarging, pulled by the extravagance of the idol. He was seeing amused faces, surprised, enthusiastic; some were looking inside of the store in order to see how he was reacting to it. This detail triggered him to get out to the street to persuade everybody that the idea of that genius was not altering his good temper at all.

Though he himself could not contain his laughing in seeing those eyes off hard egg sclerotic, solemnly bovine, were projecting upon him with an expression of a paranoiac complicity and of joyful celebration of his craziness.

Nevertheless Salvador Dalí was not laughing at all. In spite that from his frighten air of his head to the large toe in his foot he was a pure hilarity. His iron forged moustache, having its two ends curled up with a classic distinction, caused a medieval effect as a trident of an infuriated god or as the scimitar of an invader having bad fleas. In that very moment a kind of an urban thunder was produced because three troops of *paparazzi* coincided arriving to the place, belonging mainly to *The New York Times,* to *Life* and to *Daily News,* and they were stepping between the onlookers with rudeness, pushing people aside in order to clear their way and to be able to shoot their cameras at Dalí. In the avenue a knot of cars was made, abandoned by their drivers and occupants in order to go and watch that phenomenon, pushing people to the side and gaining positions as the newsmen were doing. An incredible mess had been created around the store of Isaac Goldsmith. Bullhorns were blown out in all directions, the windows of the buildings of the avenue were full of curious lookers and shooting cameras, the police sirens were heard in all the corners, and it was impossible to them to get into the impenetrable mass of people and cars. Salvador Dalí was absorbing the disaster with his open eyes, with his face marked with a dye of serious and challenging alacrity, yet triumphal behind the pugnacity of his moustache.

The elderly Isaac sent a clerk to by a pitcher of coffee to the nearest bar. And once Isaac got it, in order to be more polite, poured it out in a cup of Hittite ceramic, amphora shaped and he personally brought it, upon a small old metal dish with Moorish arabesques to the exhibited man; Dalí looked at the gift with his rotund eyes and left his stick ndwithin one of the Minoan amphoras as an emperor, to be able to handle the offer. He tasted his coffee and looked at everybody in the street, challenging one by one to perceive in the distance the taste of that affable liquid and so merited by his artistic paintings. Once the coffee was finished, threw the dish and the cop to a young lady, through that damaged show window, being the lady a young diplomat of a recently civilized and developed Banana Republic.

Once the order was reestablished and the spectacle reached its happy end, as all the things of this contingent world reach their final point, Dalí jumped to the ground of the store to get the congratulations from the boss.

"Do you know the personality who broke your window?" he wanted to know.

"Yes, I do!" the other answered with a light of satisfaction in his eyes.

"And among my excellent painting which one, do you think, is the most sublime of all?" Dalí insisted in his aspect of a painter, with great transcendence.

"*The Fainting of the Watches!*" was Isaac's short, definitive answer.

"Oh, there is no doubt that you know what you are talking about!" Dalí approved, full of a happy indifference. "So, then, bring me some canvas and a brush in order that I reproduce it for you as an exquisite compensation for the damage I have caused you. As a matter of fact a profitable damage, do you agree?" raising his finger to the curl of the moustache and rotating his large pupils.

Isaac sent the young boy to get the canvas in the gallery and was not late in coming back with the canvas. Dalí reproduced on it the painting humming *Michelle, ma belle,* of the Beatles, in an easy way. He delayed on it the lapse of time of a genius' measure. And Dalí never stopped humming some song of those in fashion at the moment. The result was a reproduction *sui generis,* between broken and perfect, yet with strange hue of suggestion which captivated the old Isaac.

Dalí looked at his piece, with tenderness for a short period. Opened the door and took off, satisfied, forgetting the painting in the ground of the store, as it was the matter of nothing relevant among the many of his genial creations in the field of pictorial dearness.

Isaac ran to hang the painting in the wall and then he had to deal with the avalanche of intruders to the store, getting in to admire it and to buy any trifle, or some of a real value, it has to be said, in order to make out of it a remembrance of the epic event. Later on he placed beside it the broken glass with the walking stick and they both became the most ambitious touristic goal in the City for a long period, while Isaac got tired of denying the sail of hose memorable items.

And it happened that the clock of the life of Isaac marked its final fainting. Because of the things of life reach their end.

And then a furious speculation about the façade of the block in the heart of Manhattan arouse, which still kept its low, miserable appearance standing up.

Before the third anniversary of the death of Isaac Smith came, several skyscrapers of iron and glass were erected and flourishing in the block of Isaac store. The fever of the speculation put aside the memory of Dali's painting, *The Faint of the Watches*. And as soon as *The New York Times* blew the gaff, a bunch of question marks about the whereabouts of the painting aroused among the citizens... The greediest satraps in the gallery business moved an intense activity to know what happened to it. The general impression was that the earth had swallowed it.

Everybody had it for granted that it was removed with the rubbish of Isaac's store, by simple workers ignorant about the sublime art of the surrealist painting.

Until today, many greedy satraps in the business of gallery, disguised as beggars, scan in the rubbish dump generated by the large town with the great hope that someday they will unearth the multimillionaire painting.

# The god of the genocide

*I*t was 7 o'clock a. m. in that frigid morning onTuesday, December 15, and the few passersby were dressed with anoraks of a quilted texture. In spite of being in Flatbush, the most crowded and of heavy transit artery in Brooklyn, and for this reason it is the most cosmopolitan containing individuals of many languages and nations. The bitter cold was keeping everybody at home and in bed it was very comfortable, enjoying the benign warmth of the blankets which the idea of the bitter cold outside was turning even more delightful.

Kemal Handal was the only man walking in the side walk with not much decided steps and rather not properly protected by clothing, since he was wearing simple mid time jacket and its thin hood. He was getting away from his uncomfortable flat in a very cheap boarding house, where he spent the night hearing irreverent music and voices of prostitutes and their lovers, implied in the practices of making love until dawn. He was looking for a place with pure air and the company of clean people, and not aggressive, where he could think and plan how he could survive in an ambient where nobody was saying hello to him, and let alone smiling to him.

Disconcerted, he leaned in a mail box in a corner. He asked himself why he was doing it... Is it because you don't feel good? But not, he was alright, his head was normal, he had not a headache, neither his belly was hurting him, he just experimented an empty stomach, which he could fill with a hot cup of coffee. He looked at the two directions of the street perpendicular to the avenue and did not see any open bar or cafeteria. He had no choice but wait for another while. In short the street would become a field of fast dashes of anonyms half sleeping neighbors, sacked, with their heads sunk to their ears, with their red noses, going to work, to get lost in the infinite swell on the City and in its infinite business places.

He doubled his anorak upon his thorax to protect it from the penetration of the cold air and his mind went far away. He saw the bulldozer approaching home as a furious monster, with the intention of crashing against his house to demolish it. He withdrew his hands from the pockets of the pan and with them made strange gesture in the cold air as he wanted to stop the monster or to dismiss the memories from his mind. But he did not get it; the big beast was going on, beat with its big device the façade of his house and it was totally collapsing with its roof; his wife could hardly scape with the baby in her arms. Then she left the little one in his hands and confronted the monster to stop it, screaming hysterically and invoking Allah in order that he saved her house. But the obstinate driver of the infamous machine ignored her desperation and applied that device to the flank of the building and demolished it all. In which moment he, Kemal, bent down to the ground to get a large stone to throw it to his head and kill him, before the eight or ten solders in the watch could stop his action.

In this point his memory fades away. He now does not

disregard that they could apply a soporific to his nose, fast, from behind... The fact was that he awaked in prison, without having a clear notion about self and feeling pain in all his body, but not being localized in any of his members. And he was there for three months, not knowing anything about his wife and his child or about the world... he was just told that his sentence was light because the stone he threw to the head of that driver was avoided by him and impacted in the iron roof of the machine.

When the door of his prison was open it was to punt him in an autobus that, with other Palestinian, drove them to a refugee camp south of Lebanon. And there he had a lot of time to think about his wife and is child, ignoring whether they were alive or dead...

Being leaned in that mail box, the bitter cold could not cool the temperature perspired by the hatred to the destroyers of his home. Against their camouflaged plan of eliminating the Palestinians from Palestine, which is their national territory, against their violence of an animal of the forest beyond the human limits. There had been an act of terrorism done by Hamas in which two Israelites solders lost their lives and the local heads of the army, thirsting for Palestinian blood, drunken off vengeance, sent three or four machines to demolish houses of innocent Palestinians at random, the first ones in their way. But neither he, or anybody else from his house, belonged to that group of terrorists! The scoundrels got the occasion to continue their job to suppress Palestinians, in Palestine. They want it for them alone, to establish on it the absolute domain of their State. And meanwhile they commit all these crimes against humanity. And the world knows it all! Yet keeps its mouth shut and keeps indifferent about it. Infamous injustice! It's an aberration of that so mentioned pacifism of the United Nations and of many altruistic associations!

Kemal realized that he was shriving because of the bitter cold in all his body, as a web of needles he had fixed all over it. He moved, he walked not knowing where. Finally, there in Lebanon, a brother of his mother –coming back to his remembering–, a strong business man in Sidon, knowing that he was in that Palestinians refugee camp, sent to him a ticket to fly by TWA to New York, with his visa of entrance as a temporal political refugee, issued by the American Embassy in Beirut. And here, in Brooklyn, he was now. Hating to death the Country which protected the despots and their unbelievable crimes and which afterwards was palliating the effects in the victims as a sign of humanity in front of the world. He would act deeply to gain power to remove the disguise from their faces and to liberate his people!

He stopped in front of a church. Several people were getting in there, not that many, and small group of nuns. When the ample door was open, some lukewarm air was coming to him with a vague scent of incense. Of course a heating system was in there. He stepped in, too. He trusted those people because they were looking all educated and good persons and so they would not refuse him because of his garment. Just one lady approached him to indicate to remove the hood of his head, out of respect to the sacred place.

He did it. He said thanks to her with a kind smile and seated in one of the last pews. He sponged his body and inhaled the fine lukewarm air of the interior. Other lights were put on in the tabernacle, where a cross with somebody crucified was presiding, where candles already were lit upon a table covered with a white cloth. Through a side door in that section a boy and a celebrant, both dressed in a tunic, appeared, with some solemnity, and they commenced an act of cult to the Divinity, since people were standing up and imitated the gestures. Kemal was relaxing in the pleasant ambient and was looking with interest at whatever the two up there were doing and the others down in the audience.

Yes, the audience was taking an active part on it, because the lady who approached him before was getting up to the tabernacle.

She moved to a rearing place in the right hand, opened a book and started reading in a loud voice: "A lecture from the book of Exodus". Here Kemal made a strange face, of fright. He had in his hands *Exodus,* by Leon Uris, and some friend made an ugly comment about it. But the lady made a mistake, and excused herself in front of the audience: "Pardon me!" And turned several sheets and continued: "A lecture from the book of Numbers". Kemal was following that text with avidity. The memory of his demolished house was upsetting him again. With the same cold blood the lady who said to him to take off the hood, was finishing her lecture saying: "People of Israel... when you reach in Canaan, the land of the Malachites, you'll destroy every house, its landlord, his children, his slaves, until his last domestic animal..."

Kemal had his breathing blocked. He could not believe such words could resound in there, in a silence and a peace which to him were aberrant and diabolic. ¿Or was it that those people were a group of hypocrites friendly to the powerful?

An abscess of indignation activated him corporally and he stood up in the central corridor. He wanted to raise a voice of protest, but nothing was produced in his open mouth but a grunt of a wounded bull. That alarmed the audience and made everybody turn around to look at him. While the celebrant was approaching to the rail of the communion, ready to pay attention to him. All of the faithful in seeing that he was wearing a similar tunic to that one Jesus Christ was wearing and the outburst of that man, were frighten by a sacred panic, as they were seeing him dismissing with a whip the sellers from the temple.

"The Malachites are my people!" at last Kemal could shout and breathe. "I was born in the same territory where they lived and I have seen too my house demolished and my family dispersed and lost or suppressed! ¿What kind of a god is this one of yours who orders some of his children to destroy other children of his?"

Kemal was inspiring fear, standing up there. He could not say any other thing. He was conscious that he had taken the speech in a place where he needed some authority to take it and the bunch of faces that were looking at him with astonishment were intimidating him, rather timid as he was. He also conceived in his mind that he was causing a serious disorder and that the police could come at any moment, which would damage his status of political refugee.

With his arms on high to express his refusal of that text, he walked to the exit door and escaped to the street where he accelerated to get away from that place and not be noticed by anybody.

He left inside a surprise and an impression so ugly that kept everybody in suspense. The lady lector, still in the lectern, was crying feeling an obscure sentiment of guilt for the outrage of that man. The celebrant was standing in the corner of the platform, trying to control his emotion and ready to fix it the best way he could.

"This man... has really expressed his feeling about this lecture" he could say at last. "Let's be careful to refuse him...! He has a point about this text... wordy to be studied. Let's be careful to despise him!"

# The Spanish Rose
# in Harlem

*I*t was Saturday night, the time to enjoy the weekly salary. The time to look for the best offerings of amusements in the many centers scattered through the borough of Harlem, more attended by those having a better festive smell. From one of these saloons, in the corner of 110 Street and Amsterdam Avenue, the notes of *There is a Rose in the Spanish Harlem* were heard, with a poster in the façade which read: *Las brisas del Caribe.* And beneath it said: *Starring the popular Nat King Cole.* Those notes were exciting the desire to enjoy, to have pleasure with the carnal shaking in the dance, or were sinking more in the boring and in the nostalgia of the far away Puerto Rico.

This last aspect affected the young and lonely Óscar Rosales, recently arrived from there, and now seated in the grade at5 the entrance to the building where his mother lived. It was the desolation infused by the sadness of being away from his friends and the used amusements on Saturday night in Mayagüez. He had but not a penny in his pocket. Though this was not the most important point of the problem, since his mother was not reluctant in giving him some money; the thing was that he did not like to spend what she was winning going to mop offices and bathrooms. And more than that, his timidity kept him inactive down there because he was not capable to bring something to the house economy, being already twenty one and after working for a couple of years as an errand boy and even as taxi driver in Mayagüez. And now he could not even work as seller of newspapers in the street, because he could not speak English.

Seated down there and with his head leaned in his fist, he was dreaming of the *brisas del Caribe,* yes, those fresh and soft winds during the hours of the warmer weather from the limitless ocean, smelling fresh oxygen and the perennial movement of the waves, winds that were missing in the streets of Harlem during that hot July. He could realize that the stones, the walls and even the persons were soil with sticky warm lymph.

Young people, boys and girls, were walking in the sidewalk in front of him, the girls dressed with the minimal clothing to cover the feminine attributions and the guys dressed in miserable ways to show their total indifference about their public appearance, saying bad words and frequently obscene words addressed to the careless girls who were tolerating all the masculine dearness of the boys, among all no consideration whatsoever to the other citizens. Óscar was disgusted about it.

As a matter of fact the long street was full of very diverse people moved by the excitement of the hour. But also there were several people seated in front of the house, forming a group Puerto Rican style, chatting, enjoying the fresh breeze, mainly women. The sensuality and even the sexuality were noticeable everywhere. Óscar was imagining everything indignant and enemy to himself. The disorder armed by Hispanic and colored people in front of a bar in the center of the block, where the beer cans were moving around and where the drug dealers were moving frenetically, ended up by bothering him to the point of not being able to stand it anymore. He was ready to stand up, but the first notes of *Spanish eyes*, resounding from some of those saloons, stopped him. He inhaled those notes. In fact he could not move from there until the songs finished completely. He finally moved with his humor more tempered and happy because even in their songs they valued the charming of the Spanish girls.

He stepped in the building singing low the song heard just a minute ago and encouraged to continue tomorrow his effort to fine some job to help the economy of the house and to be able to take his mother to live in a morally better ambient. It was late and his eyes were heavy with he weigh of the sleep. But he opened them well as soon as he saw in the vestibule three young colored men who were trying to drag a Spanish girl to the open elevator. Who got the moment of surprise of the three aggressors to run to him and look for shelter in his company. Everything was fast and elementary, and even primary; the three rotters kept the elevator opened to take the girl up, with a hand fixed to her mouth in order to prevent her for shouting for help at the moment Óscar stepped in the vestibule. He opened his arms to her and got ready to defend her; he heard that another Puerto Rican girl had been taken to a roof, in one of the past nights, and raped up there by the kind of elements now looking to take this other pray to the roof. He decided to defend her no matter how dangerous it was to his own life. The girl was looking for his protection and it was sacred and encouraging his manhood.

After the first surprise, the three rotters were approaching the couple and closing a circle around them, while uttering sarcastic expressions to the braveness of the boy and flowers to the girl. Óscar had placed the girl behind himself, to the wall, and was withdrawing a knife-dagger from his pocket, always recommended to carry when leaving to the streets of Harlem;

he pushed the device to open it and the bladder was projected ahead brilliant, neat, lethal. The attackers showed reserves about that arm, they looked at it with evident fear. Óscar was showing it to them and moving it to see which one wanted to be the first to experience it. The attackers were afraid, but did not want to manifest it, they were just looking for the good occasion, the fear of blood was keeping them indecisive. Óscar did not yield to them and was ready to punch the first to attack.

Suddenly an old man stepped in the vestibule, from the street, and was so surprised on seeing at the scene. Immediately he had two of the attackers on him, holding him and fixing a hand on his mouth to avoid him shouting. At the same time the third one tried to grasp the hand of the girl to bring her to himself, and what he got was a sever punch of the dagger that almost cut a finger of his hand. On seeing blood, the attackers rushed out to the street and ran far away, according to what people say that, when the colored attackers see blood, they fly away.

The girl, Óscar and the old man were astonished, horrified and joyful, not knowing where they were, their minds lost for a moment. The three of them moved to the elevator and each went his own way in his floor, without saying good night or happy sleep

Óscar arrived to his apartment still with the dagger in hand and the bloody blade outside, because he saw it bloody and in this way he did not like to bring it back to his pocket. His mother screamed about it.

"Óscar, what is it!?"

The boy had to seat down and take his breath to explain it. He told her the whole story piece by piece.

"Now these evil people will watch you and come upon you at any time!" she commented, terrified. "It could be good to tell the police, about It… and get far away from here, the sooner we can the better".

They decided that the following day the boy would go to the police district to explain to them everything, while she was going to work.

"I am afraid that we could carry all the guilt because we are Hispanic and do not speak English…" the mother commented to him saying good bye, fearful and as talking to herself alone.

The next morning Óscar did not like going out to the street. For different reasons, one of them being what the mother said about the police and justice for them, being Hispanic. He wanted to disregard fear, because he was not afraid. He was revolving in his mind the case of the last evening and got lost measuring its scope and its consequences, which he supposed could not be that pleasant to his mother and to him. Sometimes everything seemed to be so favorable to them, and some other times he was considering that the best they could do was to take off as soon as possible, as his mother said. Let's go back to Mayagüez the best place in the world to live, always in contact with the beautiful and affable ocean! There people are peaceful and friendly.

When the mother returned from work, he told her that he did not want to make things worse, since he considered that the three rotters would keep their villainy in absolute silence from the police, since there were a couple of witnesses so faithful.

"Mother, it is very convenient that we go back to Mayagüez this week, believe me " he said to her. We'll fight the two of us there and see how we do to survive; I am pretty sure that it will go much better than here to us over there".

The lady kept silent for the moment. She just turned her face around not to be seen crying by him. She set the table for dinner and to watch television more than talk. They had not finished dinner when the outside bell rang and the both were afraid. The mother wanted to go to open the door, but he stopped her and begged her not to move from the table. He went to get his dagger and put it in his pocket.

"Look through the whole in the door to see first who it is" she suggested him in a low voice.

But he did not even want to do it, in order not to get more afraid. Stepping firm in the ground he went to the door and opened it normally.

It was the girl he had saved the night before. She was smiling to him and serene. Timide. He was highly surprised, joyfully surprised. He could not answer her salute. In that instant he configured a reality that he could just imagine as a lightning during the danger, last night: how pretty she was!

"Please, I wanted to beg you to accompany me to the supermarket" she begged softly the boy.

This one was not yet capable to answer her. Marvelous words! They were suffocating him, they seemed to him of a limitless venture. He was feeling comforted and flattered by them to the extent that he felt accelerated the beating of his heart!

But the mother and the girl smiled to each other, because they were friends some time ago. The mother came to the door and kissed the girl.

"My son, she is Altagracia!" told the boy. "She want the price of "The Rose, Queen of Harlem", organized by our parish of The Holly Agony.

With the presence of that girl in the apartment, aunt and nephew forgot their problems and felt a true happiness, they foresaw a beautiful future, that was keeping the boy in a kind of ecstasy.

Then the two youngsters departed for the supermarket.

Óscar was so happy, he could not believe this sudden happiness having that girl under his responsibility. She was totally abandoned to his protection and care, particularity that increased his happiness, because he was feeling it in the deep of his heart. He felt the most fortunate and strong man, capable to subdue the whole world to his power.

Once he had left her sane and secure in her apartment, two up the one of his mother, he return to it and was surprised seeing under the dining room table the stretched legs and the shoes of a man. It was the old one that yesterday stepped into the vestibule when the three rotters were pressing the circle around her and himself. The old man stood up and hugged him.

He was a strong enterpriser who had five textile factories in the New York area. He was that old either, he had to be in his middle fifties.

"I need a man of honest and strong temper to supervise one of my factories where almost everybody is Spanish and you fit totally my man. At the same time you will practice your English and learn it fast" he told the boy.

Óscar, again, could not believe what he was hearing and was bravely surprised at the words of the known gentleman.

"I never make a mistake on the elements I need for my business" the old man confirmed to the mother and the son.

Once they had talked about the salary and the conditions, Óscar embraced him again, out of the impulse of his venture.

When he was gone, the nephew said to his mother:

"Now, with this job and with this salary, we'll be able to move from this dangerous place and go to some other safer and cleaner. Our families will go to live there in peace and we'll prosper a lot in life".

Saying *our families,* of course he was including the parents and the little brother of *The Spanish Rose of Harlem.*

# The Hypersensitive

That winter was bitterly cold. The cold wind was scratching the roughcast of the houses, was stiffening the poles of the electricity and was freezing to entrances to the subway. Because of the excessive demand, the steam for the heating of the houses came with so much pressure that it broke the valves of security of the underground pipes and the streets and the avenues of the large Town seamed fields of geysers pushed to the surface by the fire in the center of the earth. The winds blowing from the North Pole, and scented by the forests in Canada, were channeling in the surface of Hudson river and penetrating into the avenues, spreading the whip of the frost and pushing the citizens to the shelters. An old visionary in the nursing home of Saint Angela Merici, in the Governors' Island, declared that if he had seeing the Statue of Liberty fanning herself in the month of July to alleviate herself from the warmth in the ambient, now he was seeing her wrapping herself up sheepskin jacket from the shepherds of the Appalachian mountains deep in the night.

In fact New York was a glace mass by land and by the air. By
the air because the gables of the roofs were holding an amount of
frozen snow almost a meter thick, upon which the sunlight was
beating uselessly, since it could no melt it but yes to harden it,
exciting on it iridescence reflexes. And in the land because every
sidewalk was covered with a persistent ice layer, it is to say of
trampled snow under feet, dirty with air pollution and degraded
by junk dropped by irresponsible and careless neighbors. The
average citizen was hesitating to leave home in order to avoid that
disgusting frigid ambient and the frozen putrefaction spectacle,
which seemed to mark the final decay of the City.

It was in this occasion that the authorities got panic to the
work of the skyscrapers, which then were proving that they were
not as harmless as they looked, since they were shivering as little
one and they developed stalactites and pieces of huge ice hanging
from the gables and from the cornices and from other artistic
stony relives, like gargoyles. Walking in the sidewalks in those
days created an urban psychosis of having a permanent Damocles
sword upon your head. People were sliding to their work place, or
to the restaurant for breakfast as doing it under a death sentence,
with one eye looking up, to the top of the buildings, and the other
looking to the ground not to slide on it and open your head against
an Eskimo ax.

The fear of the citizens grew to the limits of becoming rage as
soon as the first melting of the snow started. In the hours of best
solar irradiation, the streets and the avenues were submitted to a
continuous rain of huge pieces of glace falling from the gables of
the high buildings which could become like blades of a guillotine.
It was the matter of luck, a frightening one. It was extremely
dangerous to stop in the basis of a building and those who were
going to their works, who number hundreds and thousands, were
forming a group in the center of the street, or in the opposite
sidewalk with no high building, many times getting absorbed by

the contemplation of the falling glace. They were impacting the cornices and spreading small fragments of polychromy, as they were pieces of jewelry thrown out by millionary hands. It was a spectacle wordy to be watched, it was a splendid waste of treasures!

The firemen were mobilized under a concept of even more imminence that one which claim the abundant fires of the month of July, which have to be suffocated in a drastic action in order to prevent the expanding to the other wooden buildings and finish to a conflagration of apocalyptic character. To call the firemen to extinguish… the ice!, kept everybody astonished and lost. All were mobilized in the municipal area, it is to say, all of the five boroughs, plus several others from the towns upstate and beyond the Hudson, where the high buildings are not frequent.

Those belonging to the field of fire, who never saw themselves involved in the matters of ice, anyway found the way to exhibit in front of the cosmopolitan crowds, which everywhere contemplated their work filling the streets and the avenues, making difficult the traffic in the sidewalks and in the roads, their aptitudes to fight the ice with the instruments to fight the fire. Screams and curses were heard by the walkers and those in the cars because they could not move ahead been blocked by so dense masses of human beings.

It was amazing and absorbing seeing those men up in the roofs or in the top steps of those long ladders, much upper the neighboring roofs, armed with incredible long sticks by which they were striking the ice to break it and precipitate it down the street; the fallen meteor crashing to the surface of the planet, and spreading so many pieces of brilliant ice, forced the crowds to dance a dance between crazy and macabre. Others were looking at the policemen who were in the higher windows beyond the reach of the long ladders, and from there they shut, to the open space, the point of intersection of the ice and the gable to make it fall to the empty sidewalk. And even other were looking at the men in the helicopters who were beating the ice with their sticks to make it fall in the street too.

In Forty Second Street the show was watched by a ninety years old man, seated in his armchair and through the window who, seeing those who showed their bodies through the open door of the helicopter, lost control of his emotion and rushed in his chair to the telephone, to call the City authorities.

"We are invaded by the Martians!" he shouted to the Mayor of the Town. "Now it is a fact, not a mere illusion! Move fast! We are lost!"

And these words sounded absolutely truthful in the ears of the Mayor. Who had always lived worried by the suspicion of the flying dishes, by the interplanetary voyages and by the existence of other leaving creatures in other galaxies, lords of very advanced civilizations and capacitated to undertake conquests od the unknown worlds.

Immediately all the alarms of the City were triggered at the same time. The large system of security, conceived by the most credited technicians of the Pentagon for the imminences of an atomic bombardment or in case of an invasion by strangers through the air, was on; a security system kept as a top secret as much by the Federal Authorities or by the local Authorities. The large number of very fast reactors, equipped with so potent sensors, was thrown into the air from Newark, La Guardia and Kennedy airports. They were flying in the sky of New York as humble-bees ready to shoot their deadly loads against suspicious objectives, be they human or from other planets. Prodigious gins appeared immediately in the tops of the higher buildings oriented to the outer space and were checking it with their antennas of powerful radar which discover objects at an incredible distance. People were running to the shelters or to the subway entrances under a rain of rules emitted by the speakers which were inviting them to vanish from the open air in order to save their lives. Do not delay, because it could be the end of the world! But people were stopping to look at the sky to see where finally the flying dishes appeared and to realize what the silly noise was about, I other words, the wanted to see how the Martians looked like or any others from no matter what galaxy. And they were not ready to obey any authority or to care about the death danger. First they had to satisfy the itching curiosity.

But no Martian or strange animal was any in the ambient. The only exiting fact was that the old ninety years old man, Mikhaïl Chernikov, reputed North-American spy of the Russian activities interplanetary and of the construction of Russian missiles of war, retired with $3,000.000, deposited in the branch of Chase Manhattan Bank, in the ground floor of his skyscraper, was looking threatens of assault to that bank in any activity around his building and he was persuaded that the ones who were shooting up to the neighboring roofs were doing it against the Martian who came to still his savings –the firemen who were protecting the lives of the citizens and his own. The old man did not want that what he had won with so much effort –traitor to the Country of his parents– was finally inherited by another one who was no his person.

# No oxygen in the house

*V*ilkas Valiusaitis was a Lithuanian much demanding from life. He was also demanding from men, in the same measure he was demanding from himself, plus he had a tendency to bitter his soul with the impediments caused by the human stupidity in the long run of life, which could be so easy and pleasant for all men. The impediments that the English language was causing in the daily life, for example, well could be avoided if everybody spoke his Baltic language, the Lithuanian, so easy and beautiful. He had to make an inhuman effort to assimilate those accents and the words of that fast language, so evaporated, with their velvet and sliding skin, and got angry and disappointed when people were talking to him and he could not understand them. But in cold blood he recognized that it was very useful to him that people talked to him, if he had the intention to stay in the Country. The day he arrived to the rectory of Saint Anselm, in the dioceses of New York, the housekeeper and the cook discovered his failure and surely they listed him down in their list of guys of human qualities, according to that North American endemic criteria: "No English: Nothing! No value whatsoever!"

From the beginning Vilkas could tell a part the difference of treatment between the notorious members of the community and himself from the part of the ladies of the house. His American colleagues were five in the house. And he made the sixth, yet only five were taken in account, since he did not reach the house category, his person was the low appendix that did not fulfill the entire person, because they considered him a *minus habens,* who needed guidance, control and manipulation according to his obvious human limitations. In the beginning Vilkas was aware of all these things just vaguely and he tried to put in the background of the situation his bad temper and the disgust he was experiencing, while considering his luck of having a shelter in the Country and that he had to undergo it in order to behave, work and observe the endeavor of the others to become one of them to be considered in the same line by they and by the service personal.

Silence, observation and cautiousness made the trilogy of the strategy the new man in the house imposed himself to become one of them and in the long run be normal in the daily order of the house. This quiet and easy attitude, though, was considered by those ladies more reason to be harsh and unconsidered to him and were encouraged to increment their intervention over him in the internal life, reducing the circle of "protection" around him and making him even lower at their eyes. Vilkas was keeping the vivid memory of the big disasters of the last European conflagration and he had it very soon solved: the cook was of German origin being her name Mrs. Gertrude Weis and, so, he named her *in pectore*: *The Führer;* the other lady, older than the other, was of Italian origin, Mrs. Sofia di Vitto, she was far away from the absorbent campaigns of the menstrual periods, but of a primitive endeavor and who was influenced by the spirit of the iron German one, and the Italian one Vilkas distinguished by the name of: *Il Duce.*

Gertrude, yes, was the iron chamberlain, because in few days the intelligent Lithuanian could realize that she was the secret root of the ways of life in the house, bossy, clever and with an efficient control of the soul of the pastor, an old German severe with the others and tolerant to her, with his face red as a shell of a prawn, with a voice of a judge and air of an ascetic well nourished, inflexible in the order of the ideas. The man imposed reverential awe to Vilkas, from the beginning, this one was supposing in him and iron authority and Vilkas could not understand whether he had it well impressed into his soul, or it was acting through the will of his housekeeper; Vilkas distinguished him with the name of *German Shepherd;* nevertheless he never decided to declare him the *highest* in the house.

As a matter of fact, and within the obscure law that ruled the domestic stratus concerning the principality of the guys, Vilkas realized that every time he bought and started using a couple of socks, when they came back to him, were missing in his laundry bag and could see them in the feet of the pastor –and his own substituted by others already used and almost torn. With precaution he commented it to the Italian lady, Mrs. Sofia di Vitto, *Il Duce,* who refused to listen to him, making him understand that she did not like the risk of commenting nonsenses that could ruin her relationship to the "boss".

Though where the immigrant experienced the biggest difficulties, with his phonetic and grammar was at table with the meals. This field was of the absolute dominion of *The Führer* who observed, serving food, her old habits mainly based in the junk food, the hot dogs, the hamburgers and the peanut butter and jam sandwiches, so different from the Lithuanian cuisine, this consisting in soups and broths which could be cut with a knife, meat dishes in different and wise combinations, heavy with rich accessories absolutely satisfactory to the most demanding stomachs. These nourishing handicaps kept his mind suffering, his body thin and week and his soul disappointed.

And then the problem was enlarged with the three days in the week he was going to the university to take courses on the English

language and in the Slovakian philology, and he was back for
dinner when those in the house had already abandoned the table.
Then he had to help himself with what was left in the refrigerator
from the previous dinner or take something from what *The
Führer* left on the kitchen in lukewarm platters. *The Führer* did
not cooperate at all with this penance; rather she was watching
in dissimulation, with the strictness of a Nazi guardian, molested
because the Lithuanian did not submit to her domestic law that
said "Who is absent from the table, is not taken on account". This
established a give and-take, painful at least for the poor Vilkas, it
has to be measured this way, because nobody knows until what
stratus of sadism the woman reach making him suffer and be
hungry with her hidden adversity. Vilkas could realize now and
then that some good leftovers of dinner were thrown out to the
garbage pot, to avoid he could use it.

He conceived the idea to inform the *German Shepherd* about
it, but he was afraid because he was not sure about making
him angry because he was accusing the boss of the kitchen of
malevolence against his person. Meanwhile the anguish caused by
the insecurity of having a full dinner in the evenings he was going
to the university had no solution. The cook had affirmed more
power and had realized that the last come to the house had a weak
character and was easy to control, fearing her rules in the kitchen.
The truth was that Vilkas Valiusatis was using on it the patience
of an ascetic monk and for this reason he has reduced as an ascetic
monk, as much because of hunger he had to endure those evenings
and as much because of the effort to keep moderating his impulses
and to stand firm in the place before acquiring fame of a trouble
maker in the mind of the pastor –and in the mind of those in
the chancery. In spite the fact that he knew how difficult for him
would be to keep calm and the fact that he was waiting for some
good occasion that was a revulsive of the situation to access to the
normal life the others were living in the house.

By the way, one of those days he was coming back from the university hungering and dying to fill his empty stomach. As he was approaching the rectory he was praying instinctively that some of the mates had not come in for dinner, since in this case he could get advantage of the full dish the cook used to reserve for him in the ardour. He arrived in the house when everybody had already dinner and he found the kitchen alone and with the effectives of dinner still in disorder. He saw in a pan on the ardour two roasted stakes that irradiated a gluttonous attraction and a bowl full of mash potatoes, which enamored in the same measure. He did not delay about it, he got one of the largest dishes, helped himself with the best done stake, added to it two full spoons of mash potatoes and still adorned it with two sprouts of broccoli and another full spoon of corn.

Suddenly *The Führer* appeared in the kitchen, from nobody knows where, and with a fast gesture of a cat she grasped the stake in the dish with her hand and placed it again in the pan, considering whether she was doing the same to the rest or what. Vilkas got the Lithuanian in his temper and smashed the dish in the face of *The Führer*, where it stood fixed for a couple of instants, as it happens in the American films, before falling into the ground and breaking into pieces. Immediately the stranger took off, not caring about the groans of a wounded tigress of *The Führer*, obstructed by the mash potatoes in her throat, not being able to curse him in plain voice.

Vilkas went to a restaurant that evening to fill his stomach, and late in the night returned to the rectory and escaped to his room.

The following day he prepared his suitcases early in the morning and went down to the room of the pastor, before he could get out to take care of his multiple jobs. He was seated in his desk rearing the breviary, with an aspect rather reflexive.

"I come to say far well to you and to the brothers" informed him in reference to the facts of the previous evening.

And seeing that the man did not alter his expression, that his fallen cheeks of a bulldog accused a light shiver and that the apoplectic color of his face was not alter at all, he added to it:

"I am sincerely grateful to you for all your attentions and kindness... And now, allow me to go to my way, please".

"Well" the man answer, breaking his silence and stopping him. "Yesterday you did what I had to do in twenty four years and I did not dear to do..."

And after another short silence he added:

"Please, stay here because your temper and your personality can be a good help to me. Please"

# The fat and happy stomach Buda

Lu Quen was a young Chinese boy who took part in the student riots in Tiananmen Square. He had a generous and intrepid character, he also stood in front of a tank in order to impede it to reach the companions who were lying in the pavement. He was lucky because his audacity took place in front of a photographer and in this way his image did not go around the world as a defeated one, but as a hero. He had such a strong soul that he did not fear death for the cause of freedom. He worked, while the upheaval was on, to subvert the government and to give to his people good oxygen to breath.

Nevertheless he was not silly. As soon as he saw that the power *de facto* recovered its position, he was very alert to realize on time whether they had him in the list of the ones to be purged. He continued with the routine of going to the university, but always with the alert about being in danger of being arrested.

And the situation did not last for long. One morning he was alone at home, already in the verge of departing for the university, he saw, in the long corridor between the poor barracks, several soldiers who were entering it to come to his house. Immediately Lu Quen became a young lady. With the red bag of his sister hung from his shoulder, which combined with her red dress, this one cut up down to show the pretty leg, covered with a panty hose off silk from Xian, and his lips painted with a furious red lipstick. With that not much décor for a young lady so fine, Lu Quen walked three corners, after crossing through the middle of the squad of soldiers wiggling his hips like a distinguished young lady does to claim attention from young men, and walked in the sidewalk of the main avenue to the bus that was taking him every day to the university.

There, in the vestibule, he took the most transcendental adventure of his life: abandon the Chinese territory and go to the house of his uncle in China Town, in New York, where he would start a life of liberty and work hardly to liberate his Country from the oppressors. He even considered getting involved in the key places of the North American politics to work for his ideal. He walked to the nearest train station and, on seeing a train headed for the far away Mongolia, he slide into a wagon and seated on it to relax. His first intention was get out of the scope of his persecutors. He traveled playing a game with the ticket collector of the train, sometimes hidden under the seats and other times fixed in the iron of the chassis.

And he stepped no long in the Mongolian territory since, jumping up behind the load trucks, sometimes hitch-hacking, walking and begging a piece of bread in the farms, he arrived to Moscow. At the end a long month traveling which whipped his body, but which affirmed his purpose and strung his soul. But seeing that in there they were living too under the whip of communism, he continued his trip to the free countries of the west of Europe.

He became to Berlin. He was admitted as the boss boy in a hotel-restaurant, while in his free time he was searching the most remunerated job to gather the dollars he needed to fly to New York. He found a place in one of the liners that was making voyages to the countries of the North Atlantic in America. He signed a contract as a cleaning man and as a stevedore, which was obliging him for three years.

Less than a month later his vessel tied up in the port of Newark, New Jersey. He got permission per several hours and went straight to the bus station to take one to the center of New York. Once there he oriented himself and took the subway to China Town, where he easy found the address of his uncle.

This one and his family welcome him as a hero. Yet with a reserve, that they could not offer to him their apartment because his status of *fugitive* could carry bad legal problems to them They offered to pay one for him, around their one, until he had legalized his status and got a job to survive. He agreed to it, and preferred it.

The night had come and the following morning he got in the street ready to explore the ambient. He could realize that China Town as really Chinese. Except some passerby who had inscribed in his person that he was a simple visitor and not a resident. He liked to see the relaxed persons of the Chinese people residents in the place and the vital reconciliation that his fellow citizens were breathing in America; the Chinese girls reflected in their faces that they were happy there and showed the ambition to live and prosper in life –surely in this aspect different from the ones in China under the communist rule. He looked to them with hope and ambition, and they answered to him with a smile, also unusual in his place of origin. People there looked happy and the ambient was like the one of a feast.

In fact Canal Street was a full of people celebrating something. That night it had snowed around a foot in the ground and the snowed had already being removed from the roads and placed in side where the crowd was trampling it and soiling it more and more; it seemed to be a poisonous riot, but it was not. It was a feast. People laughed and jumped at the rhythm imposed by a dragon jumping like a spirited wild beast of the forest, with its head and its tale erected and arrogant like a rational. Oh, yes, it was the 14 of February, New Year of the Chinese world! The monster was exhibiting trimmings of hairy furbelows, that shacked like in the assault of a pray, and it was variegated and feline, long and fearful. It was hostile to the mass of the attendants and loved by them. Lu Quen felt at home with that frenetic vision. He waited with patience that a couple of human feet under the huge shell of that dragon and he rushed under it as soon as the young guy who was in the tale abandoned the structure.

He grasped the pants of the guy in front of him and added the joy of his jumps to the general ones. He was pushing his head to the ass of the guy in front of him and was wondering he noticed it so soft and receptive. But he jump, jump by his feet and by his head, he was enjoying it, he was celebrating his arrival to America and taking up the ambient with such an easy way and delight; he was sure that the noise made by the ones aside was due the his superb jumps.

When twenty minutes later they arrived to the warehouse he was surprised realizing that the one he had in front of him jumping was a girl. My goodness! He looked at her with panic and she looked at him with benevolence.

"You come from the country of stress and oppressions, don't you?" she asked him.

"Yes!" he admitted. "There you could not enjoy so beautiful and human celebration, without a strict control of the soldiers or of the police. A girl never could be admitted I the "place" you were occupying".

"Equality of rights, my friend" she cooled. "Here never dissent of anything, I advised you, provided it is human".

At noon his family informed him that there was a wedding of a good friend and that he was invited to the banquet of that evening. As a well come of the Chinese colony and in order that he got acquainted with the social ambient.

When he was waking in the street as the best man of his so beautifully dressed cosine and he wearing a splendid tails, he was feeling overcome by the luxury and the big expenses the feast was implying. They were walking in Mott Street heading to Pagoda Restaurant and he was paying attention to the show windows of the minor restaurants and stores exhibiting such abundance of provisions and the number of dead animals that were marinating at the dense air of the interiors hanging upon the widows; he was thinking of the only sweet potato his family had to be share by all the members of the family. And frequently his family just had an only sweet potato to be shared in all the meals of the day. The contrast was cruel and indignant to him.

He seated at the table beside his cousin and among several friends of her, boys and girls, extraverted, liberated, not behaving a little bit of the Chinese timidity and behavior. To his astonished eyes was displayed to panorama of the aperitifs, trays with abundance of delicacies, variegated, seductive, which to him they seemed exotic, in spite that his neighbors were assuring him that they were normal, typical of the old Chinese cuisine. Everything was succulent and good to satisfy a bull. Then the noise, the joy, eating and drinking were getting scandalous in there.

And he was surprised seeing the team of the many waiters, women and men, serving in the numerous tables, bringing trays full of riche dishes. It was not finished yet with the abundance of succulent aperitifs, still was necessary to eat much more, though he was configuring his limit. Certainly, he took vengeance of the long fasts imposed by the communist party there, in China! In any how his neighbors were all normal and were ready to confront everything coming on them. Lu counted twelve different entries, four of different birds, four of fish and four of different meats. He observed that the boys tasted everything and in some dishes they were glory; and the girls did more or less the same with their almond eyes, their fine hands and a little bit greasy, emitting some sigh of saturation and of worry about getting fat. The Chinese beer, the American whisky and the European wines were abundantly consumed in the tables. Lu was doing his best, overcome, upset, yet careful not to be too different from the rest. But his head got heavy and dark, and he spent the rest of the banquet fighting to be normal at table.

His head just got clear when he saw a Buda in front of him. Ho was smiling to him with an acid face and was raising a sententious finger to him. He was a fat Buda, seated in an opulent satisfaction and perfectly reconciled to the happiness of his full stomach; Lu Quen was all confused and ashamed in front of the vision. He had stumbles in the side walk on leaving Pagoda Restaurant with his cousin and went to fix his nose to the show window of a store. Buda was blaming him for the ignominy of his crapulence, surrounded by his air of bliss and in frank offer of mystic debauchery to his faithful, which was the most painful to the poor boy. And it was so that he could not endure it and fell in the arms of his cousin, who supported him and then accompanied to the door of his apartment.

He tumbled down to his bed. He was feeling too heavy because of the excess of his stomach and upset by the sentiment of having abandoned his siblings to their awful luck, to indulge himself in the debauchery. While sleeping he saw the Buda finger in the air making summoning him; he was dreaming scenes of despotisms from the part of the powerful upon the beloved ones. Buda's finger was admonishing him that he would forget his family in China, overcome by the debauchery of the City of New York, as it happened to the other Chinese. And Buda was insisting to point him as a traitor to his people and a deserter.

While having the morning bath he tried to clean his body the infectious shadow left by the banquet of the previous day, he was ashamed to the point that he did not dare to look at the mirror and he combed his hair standing in front of the wall.

Surely that he would work for the free China from its frontier or inside of it in the underground.

And he immediately started his way back to China, vice versa he did before to come to New York. By the same system of traveling.

# The Sicilian Profile
# of the Wasp

*T*here was a trill in the ambient, individual itching and silence. The most, there were quiet whispers with a degree of poison inspired by the hermetism of the new comer and by his astute caution of not letting offer any external sign to the curiosity about who he was and for what reason he came to the place. But...was it really astute caution? Or may be discrete caution? To several of the most active in the field of the organized crime that evasive appearance was keeping everybody awake in bed. Let alone because they were convinced that the beauty was of Sicilian ascent, a recent one or since a few decades.

He came to the borough without any male or female company. (Though this detail not always is of biologic rigor in a guy who has to act with a professional egocentrism and the consistency of a bull in regard to suppress any external drainage in reference to the secret intentions he brings as far as the development of his intrigues is concern). But this detail of not bringing any female company added bewilder to the case. Giorgio Mascaro just arrived to Little Italy. But he was not coming from Palermo, everybody had it for granted, since his English was rather fine and genuine, he did not have a heavy stranger accent. The little colony was in the watch, using their best clinical means to nose around and to determine who is who in the unpredictable world, in the sudden wickedness and the plot to do evil.

Anyway, and already at the evening of his arrival, the suspicion was growing whether it could be the style of the smart, daring and easy evildoer who strikes in a place and immediately appears far away in another, where he gets smart to document his alibi –dirty trick that causes incredible difficulties for investigators and judges to prove him guilty. Many were in a thrill expecting some mischief against the local order, disturbing of the system. The new comer looked young, yet a mature guy, he had the aspect of a rich man of those who do not care about their money, though they just simulate it. Women were the most bewildered, because the known element was handsome, gracious and corpulent, silent like a fortress of those introverted, without open doors and windows to the exterior, that are so pleasant to the feminine ambition to bring them down with their love attractions. The house keepers were seen in the galleries to scold the cats, but it was to comment with the neighbor female the theme of that unknown who carried so much intrigue.

The authorities in Little Italy, who in fact are those who click the keys of everything articulated by the underground of that sector, gathered and expressed their absolute opposition to the presence of that stranger in their jurisdiction.

"Nowadays, in these evil times we have to go through, we need to know who is who among us" –the oldest counselor manifested very strict, yet a little bit lost–. "We ought to say enough to this fact that any new coming guy can be a menace to the good name of the Cosa Nostra, with his studied ambiguities as far as the practice of the crime is concerned".

"I do not even see a Sicilian air in his person" one member of the youngest pointed out, also lost and failing to be strict.

"He says his name is Giorgio Mascaro…" added one of the les experts in the system of classifying an outlaw at the first sight.

"Boloney!" an old man disagreed, who at every moment was moving his lips to say his opinion. "This is a false name! Dress him with a Scotch skirt and you'll see one of those idiots who blow the bagpipe in Saint Patrick's Day Parade, with a nose like a pepper, believe me!"

"Having in his eyes the color of the ashes!" pointed out to him another young guy of the group.

"This guy is a bloody Anglo Saxon who brings something hidden to do among us! We have to be in the watch, O. K? The most relevant trait of the Anglo Saxon culture is to strike suddenly and afterwards attribute it to the contrary, let's not forget it!"

It was the fatalist word of the first old man who had spoken, always nervous and with the panic noticeable in his skin.

They resolved to name a detective of the Cosa Nostra with the assignation to follow the steps of the new comer very closely, but without giving to him the less motive for suspicion, in order that he could act free and confident, so that in this way he could manifest the purpose of his visit.

They selected the man considered the best in the experience of the organized crime. He was the grandson of Al Capone, not considering other advantages of his character, and his experience rather stretching to the organized crime in the local, state and federal level, which surely could be desired from those more involved in the organized and not organized crime.

And something happened not registered by the chronicles, for the reason of its secrecy and the radical silence it was involved with, which took place in the most secret of the rooms in which the Salvation Army was gathering, a truly philanthropic name, yet it had hidden at least in the sector of Little Italy, the Anglo Saxon branch of the organized crime, that was fighting for the survival of the classical and conservative old American values. And its components decided as those of the Cosa Nostra decided: to name an expert detective on the organized crime to spy the unknown, just come to the place with so much intrigue. And this nomination fell on the person of Frank Doyle, grandson ofthe famous writer Conan Doyle, creator of the detective Sherlock Holmes, so much known around.

And both professionals went immediately into action.

To start they both were upset by the normality and the rest shown by their man. He was moving rarely from his flat and in the first weekend they just could list two exits, one to go buying a bulb of garlic in the supermarket in the corner and the other to go buying a manual about the growing of the Canadian magpie to the kiosk in the other corner. They both rushed to write down these details in their books of notices. Meanwhile they were keeping silent about the fabrication of explosives, domestic style, and the elaboration of an underground network of corridors in order to demolish the most important buildings of the Administration in the isle of Manhattan by means of consistent amount of dynamite, idea that was panicking the two societies in the watch about the case. "Be careful and move with extreme precaution, because the evil mind of the Anglo Saxon world against the Latin culture has no limits!" those of the Salvation Army were saying to their disoriented man.

Both detectives became more lost when they saw the stranger leaving home wearing a *streimel* and the black overcoat of the Hasidim and was heading straight to a synagogue, three blocks away from his house. They both got too into the Jewish temple, not knowing either about the other, and could see their persecuted guy seating in a bench, as one among the many, and was ready to listen to a rabbi who was commenting passages of the Talmud. And their surprise was so great when they heard the preacher introduced the new comer to the temple, Giorgio Mascaro, and invited him to come up to the lectern to express a salute message to all the brothers. What the requested made speaking a perfect English, including on it some obscure expressions, which well could belong to the Modern Hebrew, since the listeners understood them with a perfect relaxation and visible internal peace.

"So, our man is a Zionist who has come to our borough to plot against the interest of the Cosa Nostra!" the elderly Moglione, head of the local branch, commented. "We need to be very careful, since we have a formidable enemy within our house!"

And more or less the same commented Mr. Oliver Fuse, President of the association Salvation Army, in front of the attendants to the local assembly.

After a couple of days, the two men in the constant watch saw the same guy getting in the street covered with a monumental Mexican *charra*, armed with a guitar and dressed as an impeccable *mariachi*, with the other detail of a creole mustache, big and black pouring out Mexican black light. They followed him without knowing one about the other doing the same. The man walked to the north of the island, pulling to him the attention of the passersby, while he walked in perfect peace, installed under the shadow of the generous *charra*. By the way more than one fellow Mexican encouraged him to patriotism on the sidewalk, shouting to him with no reserves: *¡Ándele, manito!* His itinerary was long and happy for all; he walked to the east of the Sixteenth Street and entered the church of Saint Ignatius of Loyola, of the Jesuits priests. Boys and girls of different ages were celebrating some feast there and making noise, all dressed in the tropical fashion, mainly Aztec, Mayan and Quixé. Both detectives rushed to ask what the celebration was about and the answer was "to celebrate the Mexic classification for the world championship of the fight of roosters, after defeating the proud and powerful team of the neighboring Guatemala. The Sicilian one joined a group of *mariachis* who plied the guitar and sung, with the *charra* in the ground and leaned against their bodies, the *charras* reaching to their cinctures. At the end of the ceremony the strange *mariachi* expressed a message to the attendants, which was accepted with jot by them, but not by the detectives who could not grasp but a scrap from his Spanish, yet he was speaking it so easy. They were disappointed because in such a big celebration there was not a final implication with the organized crime.

In front of this specific news, the counselors of each side, from the Salvation Army and from the Cosa Nostra, stored round in their seats, nervous, disappointed. That guy was scoffing them as a champion of the chaos. For this reason he was very dangerous and unpredictable and had to be watched carefully, never trusting him, at least until they could verify what was his ultimate intention coming precisely to Little Italy. Both detectives receive a prize for their job and were greatly encouraged to keep doing it.

The next occasion they could find him was in the Alleluia House, the hospital for the sick of aids, provided by the City. He was wearing some torn jeans, he offered signs of hunger, he had reduced, looked at the sick ones from behind a mist that was the effect of a general decay. Everything suggested that the guy was starting the final span of his existence. The color of his skin was white, but he hardly was different from the black more defeated who were in beds.

On listening to this new, the elderly lost their tempers. "It's enough!" shouted the two most elderly of each association, beating the table with their fists. The others not having this authority, livid, obstructed, were panicking since none of the wisest in the group were giving any solution about the case of that disturbing guy. "We will not allow them to upset us because of some dirty tricks meant to confuse us!" the elderly of every side shouted. "The religious farce and the altruistic one do not make us forget that the beauty has his hands stained with blood!" the elderly concluded, separated one from the other, yet almost at unison.

The two councils reach the end of their endurance. And each one decided to take a final action that had to establish a final period to the upset temper of all the presents in regard to the cunning guy who was making fun of them with so ignominious tricks.

Those of the Salvation Army decided to send their expert to the guy to assail him and get his documents –identification card, passport, secret letters– or to provoke him to define who he was, why he came to the borough of Little Italy, and why his disappointing conduct to confuse them.

And those of the Cosa Nostra did the same, though vice versa. They begged their man to use the friendly approach and to provoke him to define his person in all the aspects of his devious conduct and, in case he was rebelling against it, then yes, use the pistol against him and forced him to deliver all the documents he carries.

Both detectives headed to Alfa building in the Fourteenth Street. They met in the vestibule and they had for granted that *the other* was one of the inmates of the building. And both stepped into the elevator and pushed the button of the fifth floor. One of the two was considering that it could be that they lost track of the first guy who came to Little Italy with so many movements back and forth... The fates of life, they both walked to apartment 5D and, when they thought that *the other* would walk beyond it to visit some other apartment, they both coincided in front of the same one. They pretended not to notice *the other* and they split.

The grandson of Conan Doyle took the elevator to the ninth floor and waited until *the other* vanished. This one got down to the garage of the building in the ground floor and left to the street to study the configuration of the fire escape. He ascended on it to the fifth floor, tried the window of a room of the apartment and saw with satisfaction that it was not fixed inside and he could raise it. He got into the room.

The grandson of Al Capone, on seeing the field free of undesirable people, stood in front of the door and, no thinking well what he was doing, shouted like in a routine: "The police!" while aiming his pistol at the door. Immediately he kicked it with violence of the apartment 5D, opened it and stepped in. Two shuts resounded and two men fell in the ground.

Shortly later the federal police came to the place to find the two dead men at the door of the apartment, each with a pistol in his hand. There was a hanging poster in the wall just upon the two cadavers which read:

"Neither the MAFIA or the WASP will stop the crimes of the underground. Just the work of Jesus Christ will do it, carried out by the Delegates of the United Churches".

"The MAFIA: Mothers and Fathers Italian Association" one of the policemen commented, with sarcasm, as he was reading it.

And the other commented:

"WASP: Vèspa, in Italian, develops into: White Anglo Saxon Protestant! In other words: The Ku-Klux-Klan, my brother! And he was reading it, with sarcasm.

# The most
# unexpected lottery

*A* crowd of fans to the opera were waiting in the staircases in the vestibule of the Metropolitan Opera, talking upon the red carpets that offers an aristocratic step. They formed an extensive and cosmopolitan group of curious elements who were anxious to see celebrities and study them. The opulent couple, shining with merits, were getting in not waiting in the stairs for anybody, but being object anyway of the scrutiny of those who waited, trying to discover their peculiarities, the wealth, the eccentricities, their dresses. The star of the cinema was jumping the stairs behind a generous low neck which almost blinded her, shaking her body exquisitely within the tied silk dress, as the snake moves within its skin.

Down, in the side of the stair, were taking four petroleum magnates, with their heads covered with the square wooden piece which presses the *kilaba* to the skull and dressed with the tunics which suggest millions of dollars; the oldest, and taller one, was imposing to behave to the other three in the middle of the noisy confusion, as his own black as a cavern mustache was giving the good example to them. "Mustafa Afif Alipatxa, to the telephone, please!" the usher shouted from the door of a cabin of telephone and the main man of the group moved to that direction with his halve angry face, because his name was ventilate upon the crowd and the other happy halve because they were doing it. All in all was a cheap, coarse propaganda montage. That evening they were presenting *Lucia de Lammermoor,* by Gaetano Donitzetti, and those who were anxious to see the *diva* Phyllis Johnson, the soprano protagonist of the opera, had to keep quiet their anxiety, since their idol did not circulate between the outstanding of the high life, but entered in the house through an excused door.

Phyllis Johnson was a lady of African origin who was honoring her race, being sculptural, having a harmonic body, with her feminine attributes placed with incredible strength in their insertion, just meant for the hypothetic and exclusive palpation by princes, magnates and pharaohs. Up in the stage her figure was impressive wearing a red dress of the color of fire from branches of the baobab, rubbed with grease of nandu, reaching to her feet and showing the black of her skin under the powerful light of the hidden focus on the sides of the stage; she was structured under a sample of a caryatid of the temple of the goddess Osiris. Her song was a bath to the listeners, sonorous, tender, chaste, potent, which implied an absolute hoarding for men, it's to say, a notorious visceral unrest, and a knowledge of primacy and uniqueness from the part of women: all of them would like to be in her place and withdraw to herself the admiration of so many men, to be owners of those accents to spell the man of their lives. The enamored bridal was standing with ardor on the posts of the stage and was flooding the orchestra and the stage-boxes with her beatings of heart translated into plethoric trills, being she always so elegant, efficient and bright. The audience was listening to her with their hearts stopped, not to disturb with its beatings the spell of her mythical enrapture.

Mustafa Afif Alipatxa was never taking his eyes away from her. He was making some groan in the middle of his little court of rivals, servants and flatterers. Those big, bovine, paranoiac eyes, were like a flame contemplating the soprano, to each movement and to each inflection of the song she was making were rotating, advancing and lighting as the socket was not handling them, as they could suddenly jump out and go the hug the singer and take her with them. The Arabian beat de mouth of his neighbor, with his fist, because he dared to bend into him and comment something idiot about the beauty of the *vedette,* in order that he was quiet and relaxed. The audience got three times the occasion a short rest of the soprano to shout bravos to her and he also raised his body and applauded like a frenzied crazy one, making three inflexions of his tors who would reach the floor as the Muslims do to the direction of the Mecca, but the benches were in his way to do it.

Finally, on seeing that he could not do it, that he could not succeed to center his person in the center of the iris od the *diva,* gave five bills of $100.00 to that neighbor of his and sent him to buy the most beautiful bouquet he could find. And the man did not delay to be back, buried under a bunch of flowers really containing the most antipode ones, which he moved upon the heads of many in the suffering audience in the moment the soprano was bending to the public thanking them for their applauses. Mustafa Afif Alipatxa grasped the bouquet from the hands of the tough guy, rebuffing him, and threw it to the feet of the singer, meaning that he would be much more happy throwing his person there; as a matter of fact, those seated behind him saw him as a ragged bird which wanted to get a pray, object of his canine hunger. The lady was getting the bouquet from the floor of the stage, embraced it and looked for the first time at the fiery magnate who sent it to her, making him a reverence. The man fell into his seat, defeated by his good fortune.

When the performance was over, the group of the four of the petroleum moved to verify the where-about o Phyllis Johnson and avoid what happened before fading away through an excused door. They used on it a nervous, fast and perspired frenzy. Mustafa Afif Alipatxa punched more than one rib with his fist and sent a servant to each door with the recommendation to be very careful not to be noticed and of observing well where the soprano was heading for, in order to be able to follow her not making any noise. For himself he reserved the area of the vestibule, where he placed himself in a discrete and strategic angle to be able to see whether she was leaving there or not.

Before he got tired of waiting he discovered his heroine in corridor coming up to the vestibule; he dissimulated his anxiety but got ready to smile to her in order that she could realize the immensity of his fire to love her. It was even increased on seeing her with the same long dress and bundled with a shawl of the color of the flame of burning petals of gardenias, which was fluffy like sugar blown in a stall. Now she was accompanied by two young black girls, tall, serene, done in the same shape as hers.

Mustafa Afif Alipatxa saw them leaving the opera building, moving his tongue under the black and hungry moustache, could see how Phyllis was telling to the driver of a car to wait for them, while the three of the were walking in the sidewalk. The four magnates of the petroleum at that time were standing in different angles to see where the young ladies were heading to. They got in a restaurant of the Columbus Circle and they rushed and stepped in the same restaurant, one by one not to be noticed.

Phyllis and the two companions seat in a table and immediately started talking; they picked a cigarette from the case offered by Phyllis, they lit it and waited for the waiter to approach. The same did the four Arabs, seated in a table in straight projections to theirs. Mustafa Afif Alipatxa selected a chair from which he could see the soprano, the object of his torment, and be seen by her without any impediment. He was extremely serious, with the moustache presiding any aspect of his face, while admonishing his mates to behave, to satisfy their concupiscent looks in other tables, since he was not ready to cause the impression in the hall of being a group of cavemen who cannot control their belly. He showed his fist to them in order that they understood how ready he was to smash it in their mouths.

He reserved the looks to that table in question to himself. Though he administered them again with brains and wisdom; first he bowed his head to her, with control and politeness, and he was answered in the same measure. This encouraged him and thought that his strategy was starting well and promising a happy end. Afterwards, in the course of the dinner, he looked at that table just now and he, with a moderate attitude not to get bothersome or to be refused, but every time he did it, he wanted to be seen in order to prepare her heart to please him.

When the time for desert came, Mustafa Afif Alipatxa considered that the algid moment of his plan arrived and asked from the waiter a small tray to offer presents to somebody. When he had it, he withdrew a golden ring from his finger that had incrusted a valuable diamond as large as a quail egg and order the boy to bring it to the soprano. He warned the boy to be careful with a $100.00 bill that was under the tray for him.

The three young black girls on seeing the jewel, exclaimed "Woooooow!" surprised and blinded by it. But not that much from the part of Phyllis, the truth has to be said, since immediately she moderated his face of admiration, showed a shadow in her eyes and wiped herself calmly with the napping, though always looking at the diamond. Slowly, with much prudence, she raised her eyes and fixed them in the person of the man who was looking intensively at her and at her reaction, with a greasy smile under his adipose moustache saturated of meat and of alcohol, but hungry for sex. The smile insinuating the Arab theory included in the present consisting in the donor expecting the distinguished one in his bed that very night. The soprano lowered her eyes to the table, with politeness.

Once they had their coffee, accompanied with small cup of anisette Marie Brisard, the three young girls abandoned the table, with a dignified solemnity that remembered the solemnity in the opera performed shortly before. Relaxed, discretely fed, fascinating, vital, with a soft tint of pink in their faces. They stood in the sidewalk in semicircle, waited there a couple of minutes, not looking at any place or caring about the ambient around, and got into the Lincoln Continental that came to pick them up. And they took off from the place.

Immediately the quartet of the black gold hurl down to the roaming door of the kitchen through which the waiters got in and out. And inside there an argument burst, with angry and strident voices which alarmed many in the dining room, in the kitchen or amused many others. They were shouting within there as they had to crush the world.

And the reason was that Phyllis Johnson, before getting up from the table with her companions, had given that ring with the diamond as an egg quail, to the waiter who already got the benefit of the $100.00 bill.

9 781480 893276